The People-Profit

CONNECTION

How to Transform the Future of Construction by Focusing on People

4th Edition

By
G. Brent Darnell

PRAISE FOR BRENT DARNELL
AND THE PEOPLE-PROFIT CONNECTION

"In the distant future, perhaps we won't need people to build projects. Until then, however, we need to pay close attention to what Brent has to say. His systematic take on the concept of emotional intelligence is not only worth looking into, it also compels us to explore that mysterious region of the project business: the people jungle. It's gotten too expensive to play ostrich when people problems infect the project team. Brent's approach can help each of us to know that:

We have a people problem.
We can isolate the cause of the problem.
We can help fix the problem.

It's true – people can change and change for the better. And applying emotional intelligence techniques can facilitate that change.

Brent has three histories going for him:

1. Brent learned his first lessons from his dad, Bob Darnell. Bob was a real leader in the construction business and helped people solve their problems using the personal approach. I know because I learned a lot from Bob, too.

2. Brent's in-the-field experience. He's been immersed in the school of hard knocks.

3. Brent's professional experience in applying emotional intelligence for a multitude of clients. Dig in, and you will gain new insights into getting things done in our people-driven world."

Gary Draper,
Draper & Associates

"Brent's enormously readable book demystifies the concept of emotional intelligence and links people skills and success in the construction industry - in fact, in any industry. A definite 'must read'."

Lisa Fanto,
Vice President, Human Resources,
Holder Construction Company

"Brent has helped me better understand my weaknesses and more importantly provided advice and tools that I could work on to improve in these areas. Brent has a rare ability to recognize each individual's area for improvement and provide guidance that is clearly understood and easily accepted. Brent has made a significant impact on both my career and personal life and I appreciate that I have been able to work with him."

Kevin Appleton,
Senior Vice President, Batson-Cook Company

"Having Brent work with our company changed our organization from the inside out. He helped us establish a vocabulary across our organization that enabled seasoned (and hardened) superintendents to relate better to their teams and their clients. Brent showed our people that it's okay to have feelings and even more okay to respect other people's feelings. We still have a lot of work to do but we now have individual plans to help us become better employees and better people."

Matt Rich,
Vice President, Jacobsen Construction

"Brent and his program have been one of the most successful and effective that we have instituted. We have identified our next generation of Leaders in the company and worked with Brent to develop those individuals to step into their 'next role' with the company. In every case, each of those individuals has stepped up their game. Brent is relentless, but tactful in pursuing the areas of improvement with our folks on a very personal basis."

Mark House,
Managing Director, The Beck Group

"We believe that relationships are our greatest asset. Brent's book takes this central idea, practically applies the concept of emotional intelligence, and offers real solutions to many industry problems. I would recommend it to any construction professional."

Jim Griffin,
CEO, R.J. Griffin & Company

"Construction has always been a people business, but the human resource challenges of the new millennium have industry players scrambling like never before to capture and utilize talent. Brent Darnell has produced a great handbook for anyone in the construction industry who wishes to elevate their understanding of the human dimension."

Hank Harris,
Senior Chairman, FMI Corporation

"Brent's book, *The People-Profit Connection*, has been well received by our managers; they describe it as 'on target' for our industry. We use emotional intelligence concepts to support our talent management work, and this book is particularly helpful in making the ideas practical in their application: better relationships produce better business outcomes."

Dr. Pam Mayer,
Succession & Development Manager,
Granite Construction Inc.

"You hit the nail on the head."

Dr. Wayne Clough,
former President, Georgia Institute of Technology
and Secretary of the Smithsonian Institution.

"Brent Darnell's book provides a critical link to creating high performing and motivated teams by helping us understand Emotional Intelligence. It will help you to create a climate where you can articulate a shared mission that moves people and, ultimately, create successful projects."

Bruce D'Agostino,
former Executive Director, Construction Management Association of America

"Every developer needs to read this little book. Recognizing that our emotional skills control our behavior, Brent identifies the key to great success – care as much about the needs of your team as your own – it's just too simple to be wrong and it applies to so much more than business."

Lou Conti,
VP, Development,
Cousins Properties Incorporated

"Brent Darnell's book makes a very subtle but dramatic point – emotional intelligence is relevant to performance in every job and any industry! He offers compelling stories and powerful insights. The book is full of ideas for improving individual and organizational performance by tapping the power of emotion."

Kate Cannon,
Emotional Intelligence Pioneer

"Brent Darnell's book accurately depicts the construction industry's reality and its need to change. More importantly, it identifies the emotional skills required to be successful in changing the industry and provides a direction in which the industry must go. In my opinion, without a focus on emotional intelligence, the industry will continue on a slow decline."

Joe Andronaco,
Founder and CEO at Access Green

"Brent Darnell breaks down the most complicated part of our business – the human psyche – into useable and quantifiable

steps in The People-Profit Connection. The process of placing people in the right positions, and training employees to enhance their people-skills is simplified by using emotional intelligence. This leads to a Win-Win situation with happier employees and better company margins. What more could anyone ask for?"

Rick Alcala,
Construction Consultant

"Brent's book is a good example for all the companies that want to be better. It shows in a very understandable way how companies can change just by paying REAL attention to their people, which is the only possible way to be different and to become the best."

Josep Sala i Teixidó,
sales manager Spain, Greece, Latin America,
Poggenpohl Möbelwerke GmbH
(A member of the Nobia group)

"Mr. Darnell's book deftly explains the complex psychological factors that govern personal relationships in a simple set of readily understandable layman's terms called 'Emotional Intelligence.' It shows how improving these people skills at every personnel level affects business performance in intuitively obvious, but often overlooked, ways. I recommend it to anyone interested in smooth, safe, and profitable construction."

Bailey Pope,
AIA, VP Design and Construction,
Harold A Dawson Company

"The book is a gem! Easy to read and understand, practical and hands-on."

Margareta Sjölund,
PhD, founder of Kandidata

"I believe there is a great deal of substance in the approach to utilizing emotional intelligence as a basis to bring about positive changes in Construction Professionals."

Tracy MacDonald,
Project Director, McCarthy Construction

THE PEOPLE-PROFIT CONNECTION

BDI Publishers · ATLANTA

Back cover photo courtesy of the Construction Management Association of America.

Cover design and layout by **Tudor Maier**

The Audio Book, read by **Lisa Leonard** (*lisa@lisaleonardvoiceworks.com*), is available on CD Baby. Visit *brentdarnell.com/shop* to purchase and download.

TABLE OF CONTENTS

Dedication

This book is dedicated to my parents:

Bob Darnell, the builder of bridges between people and places, who taught me how to get along with my fellow man,

and Betty Darnell, the life of the party, who never met a stranger.

ACKNOWLEDGEMENTS

I want to thank my wife, Andrea, for all of her encouragement and support. Her partnership and input into our Total Leadership Program has taken the results for our participants to a whole new level that changes people's lives and transforms companies. My appreciation also goes to Kate Cannon for her right-on comments, mentoring, and friendship. I also want to extend a big thanks to all of the program participants who have started their journey toward personal mastery. Thanks also go to the individuals and companies who took the leap of faith and embraced this work, especially Lisa Fanto, the Vice President of Human Resources at Holder Construction. To those companies who have agreed to share their case studies, I am eternally grateful.

FOREWORD TO THE FOURTH EDITION
BY BRADLEY PHILLIPS,
MANAGING DIRECTOR, THE BECK GROUP

In 2015 I met Brent Darnell for lunch to explore how he could help me develop the next leaders at The Beck Group. After a long lunch I knew I had found "my guy". The funny thing is, my guy turned out to be a "couple", as Brent had teamed with his wife Dr. Andrea Robbins. We ended up getting double what we were looking for.

So, "What is so special about a team that develops leaders"? Well, first of all, Brent has spent his whole career and specifically the last fifteen years refining his approach to leadership and how Emotional Intelligence plays a major role. He then teamed up with his lovely wife Dr. Robbins to emphasize the health aspect of leadership. And guess what? The health aspect is KEY!

Our next leaders are saying that this program is "life changing", because to be a great leader you have to be prepared in so many ways. No one has ever discussed the role that emotional intelligence, health, nutrition, and exercise play in your development.

The spotlight burns the brightest on the leaders. You have to be ready; mentally, physically, emotionally, and spiritually. Brent and Dr. Robbins have helped me change the course of history at Beck by preparing our next leaders better than I dreamed possible before that long lunch.

INTRODUCTION

"God gave us so many emotions, and so many strong ones. Every human being, even if he is an idiot, is a millionaire in emotions."

Isaac Bashevis Singer

"Above all else, guard your heart, for it affects everything that you do."

Proverbs 4:23 (NLT)

"When the human species has learned to harness emotion, we will be ready to take the next evolutionary step."

Charles Darwin

This book was written specifically for the AEC (Architecture, Engineering, and Construction) industry, but the more I talked to people outside of the AEC industry, the more they confirmed that these issues were applicable to many industries and businesses. This is especially true of service industries where the employees are technically educated or trained, such as engineering, healthcare, legal, information technology, telecommunications, manufacturing, the energy sector, finance, and accounting.

They all have similar problems that relate directly to their collaborative, service-oriented nature and the employees' need to effectively deal with people. By addressing these people issues, projects can be more successful and satisfying and organizations can be transformed, become less problematic, and add more to their bottom line results. In fact, if these concepts work for the AEC industry, which is generally slow to embrace change, they will work for any industry.

Imagine for a moment a brilliant future for the AEC industry where highly respected managers balance their toughness, assertiveness, and independence with highly effective interpersonal skills. Imagine an industry that is completely service-oriented and customer focused, with zero defects and total customer satisfaction for all project stakeholders. Imagine an industry where there is trust, communication, and teamwork among the owners, facility managers, end users, construction managers, architects, designers, contractors, trade partners, vendors, and suppliers.

Imagine an industry where all projects are completed ahead of schedule and well within the budget, where collaborative project delivery is the norm, where employees are respected and encouraged to thrive, where productivity skyrockets, and profit margins increase dramatically. Imagine an industry where sustainable construction is just the way we do business, where the industry's processes not only do no harm, but also contribute to a healthier planet.

Consider the power of communication and teamwork so widespread that project teams love to come to work each morning, where relationships are so strong and concern for others is so pervasive that people look out for each other and working safely is as natural as breathing. Imagine a diverse workplace that draws millions of young men, women, and minorities because they want to be a part of this wonderful business.

Imagine an industry where people reach their maximum level of performance mentally, spiritually, physically and emotionally, thrive during their career and retire full of health and vigor. Imagine an industry where we all work together to build something, to create something from nothing. That is the industry I want to be a part of, that is waiting to be.

But the big question is, "Why isn't the industry like that now?" It's a very good question. One that deserves an answer. In fact, that is the purpose of this book – to determine how the industry can transform itself into the one I have just described. There are many seemingly unsolvable problems that prevent us from having such an industry. I'm sure you are thinking of those problems right now. The first step toward solving these complex issues is to find their root causes. Once we do that, we can begin to find solutions.

I have asked successful construction people about these problems and have heard many different responses, but the common denominator seems to be related to difficulties with people. One person joked, "If it weren't for the people, this would be a fun business." When construction professionals were asked where they spend the majority of their time, they replied, "Dealing with people problems." Ask yourself this question: Are most of your problems process-oriented or people-oriented? The answer is obvious. We all know that this is a difficult industry, an industry made more complicated by the myriad of problems associated with this human dimension, which probably goes back to the building of the pyramids.

The dilemma is that no one has come up with an effective way to solve these people problems, until now. This book explores the most difficult AEC industry problems, provides some insight into their root causes, and shows how to go about solving them. And when your company solves these problems, your bottom line will dramatically increase. In order to address people issues, it is logical that we examine the people. That is where emotional intelligence comes in.

What is emotional intelligence? One simple definition is "social competence". A more in-depth definition is understanding and managing your emotions, and understanding and managing the emotions of others for the best outcomes. Sometimes that means being assertive and sometimes that means being empathetic. True emotional intelligence is knowing when to do which thing to which person at which time. The old Alabama football coach, Bear Bryant said it best: "Some kids need a pat on the back. Some kids need a kick in the butt."

By cultivating this high level of personal mastery, we are able to deal more effectively with others. This can be a difficult but worthwhile process. As Lao Tzu said, "Mastering others is strength. Mastering yourself makes you fearless." Using emotional intelligence as a foundation, you can measure and improve people skills and solve people-related problems. Teaching people skills to contractors and engineers using emotional intelligence is something that I am passionate about, and we have been doing that since 2000. During our programs, there is also focus on mental and physical peak performance, which affects everything we do.

At the beginning of this journey, when I told my wife I was going to teach emotional intelligence to architects, engineers, and contractors, she said I was crazy. How in the world could I teach these tough construction managers about emotional intelligence? Even I had my doubts. How would they react to learning about their own emotions and the emotions of others? The initial reactions, which are now predictable, were apprehension, skepticism, and resistance. They were also skeptical about how their physical well-being related to their success.

But once these initial reactions were overcome, and participants realized that emotional intelligence and their physical well-being and performance was something that could be quite important for their career development and personal lives, virtually all of them embraced the concepts. And once they embraced the concepts and worked on their emotional intelligence and peak mental and physical performance, the results were nothing short of remarkable.

As one participant put it, "I was apprehensive about this type of training in the beginning. However, after completing the course and seeing my own personal growth, I realize that the effort given has netted significant results." Another participant said, "There were times when I felt like the Karate Kid. I kept asking myself, 'Why am I continuing to 'wax on, wax off'?' But in the end, the lessons really paid off."

Another participant put it this way: "In the beginning I was a bit skeptical of how much the program could help, but after some honest soul searching and opening my mind to some unconventional (for a construction guy) techniques, some big changes were made. The program, along with some diet alterations, helped me change some long-standing problems that has helped me tremendously with my life and career."

A Senior Vice President for a top 200 contractor said, "When you came in to talk to me about this approach to management training, I was intensely skeptical. But overall, I don't think you can get through the classes without greater awareness. And that awareness leads to behavioral change. We see that on the back end with how we manage our people, turnover numbers, and morale." It is significant to note that 90% of our testimonials begin with "I was skeptical in the beginning."

This focus on the people side of business is nothing new. The introduction to Dale Carnegie's *How to Win Friends and Influence People*, which was published in 1936, states: "Research done a few years ago under the auspices of the Carnegie Foundation for the Advancement of Teaching uncovered a most important and significant fact, a fact later confirmed by additional studies made at the Carnegie Institute of Technology. These investigations revealed that even in such technical lines as engineering, about 15% of one's financial success is due to one's technical knowledge and about 85% is due to skill in human engineering, to personality and the ability to lead people."

When I first started working with emotional intelligence, my skeptical engineer's brain had many questions. You will likely have similar questions and challenges as well. This book will answer your questions and give you a path to follow. We will discuss the basics of emotional intelligence and why it is vital to your future success and the success of your company. By using the methodology outlined in this book, you will be able to develop and improve your emotional intelligence and make your life better at work and at home. For companies, you will be able to help your people be the best that they can be, solve the problems that continue to plague your business, increase your bottom line results, and maximize the success of your projects.

Chapter 1

AN INTRODUCTION TO EMOTIONAL INTELLIGENCE

"People do not remember you by any intellectual idea or concept you may have given them, but by some subtle emotional impression you may have made consciously or unconsciously. It is what one thinks about you after you have left him that counts."

Frances Wilshire

"People will work harder for someone they like, and they like you in direct proportion to the way you make them feel."

Irwin Federman,
a partner at US Venture Partners

What makes a great leader? Think for a moment about a great leader whom you admire, someone you really look up to. What are the characteristics that make this person great? Whenever I ask this question, I usually get a long list of skills. A great leader has good communication skills, empathy, listening skills, passion, assertiveness, optimism, focus, decisiveness, motivation skills, relationship skills, and vision. Invariably, it is a long list of the so-called "soft" skills, or emotional intelligence competencies. Very rarely does anyone say that a great leader has incredible technical skill or vast intellect or an advanced degree from a prestigious college.

Isn't this list of attributes just as valid for most areas of the construction business? Think of the best owner's representative, the best architect, the best designer, the best construction manager, the best laborer, the best carpenter, the best plumber, the best electrician, the best superintendent, or the best project manager.

Don't most of them possess good people skills? Aren't these people skills a vital part of what makes them effective and what makes you want to work with them? Don't we continually receive requests for our best people, the ones who have these great interpersonal skills? Isn't it a shame that we can't put them on all of our projects? If people skills differentiate these stars, then why don't we try to cultivate these skills in all of our employees?

The foundation for these wonderful people skills is emotional intelligence, and we can't escape it. Our brains are hard wired for emotions. Even our decisions are based on emotional responses. The choices we make, the red Mustang, the dark woman with red hair, that favorite pair of blue jeans, even something as simple as how you like your eggs are triggered by emotional impulses. In fact, recent brain research reveals that the emotional part of the brain is involved in every aspect of our day-to-day thought processes. Without this connection to the emotional part of the brain, cognitive thought processes such as decision-making are impossible.

Even information that we perceive with our senses is filtered through the emotional part of our brains, coloring it with our perceptions, our past experiences, and values. Because of the way we process this information, we do, truly, create our own reality. There is a story of a family that was thinking of moving to a new town. They stopped at the local gas station in the prospective town and asked the attendant about the people there. They asked him what kind of people they were. The gas station attendant asked them what the people were like in the town that they had left. They told the attendant that the people in their former town were mean, petty, and selfish and that was the reason they were leaving. He told them that the people in the prospective town were exactly the same: mean, petty, and selfish. The family drove off to the next town in search of a new place to live. The attendant knew that the family created that reality, and it would be the same no matter where they moved.

I have a personal story about how emotions, specifically optimism, created a desired outcome. The main thing we teach is how to manage your emotions for the best outcomes. I am known to be overly optimistic. I score high in optimism and low in reality testing. My wife calls me "optimistic to the point of ridiculous". I was in Sweden teaching a course for a week. Keep in mind we were out in the middle of nowhere right on the Baltic Sea. On Monday evening, after a nice sauna, I jumped into the Baltic, which was around forty-five degrees, and lost my glasses. I didn't have a backup pair of glasses or a pair of contacts. This was a disaster. I couldn't see the screen to teach and had a hard time conducting the training sessions.

I called my wife and told her about my glasses, and she contacted my optometrist and had my glasses prescription sent to the conference center. In the meantime, I told my wife that I would try to find someone with a diving mask or goggles so that I could dive down into the forty-five degree water and find my glasses. Without my glasses, I was not sure I could see well enough to find them. But I was undaunted. My wife thought this was ridiculous on two levels.

One, we were in Sweden. Who is going to have diving equipment? Two, the Baltic has tides. There is no way those glasses are going to be there after several days. But, I was undaunted.

I talked to the bartender at the conference center, who told me that she had just returned from a diving trip in Egypt and had a pair of diving goggles. She said that there was a small glasses boutique in the village where I might be able to get some contacts. And if I had contacts, I could use the goggles, dive down into the forty-five degree water and find my glasses. Keep in mind that time was passing. It was Wednesday now. I managed in the classroom, but could not drive into the village on Wednesday because of something we had to do as a class that evening.

I went to the glasses boutique with my prescription on Thursday afternoon and they had contacts for me. Thursday evening, I went back to the conference center with my contacts in and the diving goggles in hand. But it was too dark to look that night. I would have to wait until Friday.

Friday morning came, and I put on my bathing suit, my contacts, and my goggles. All of the participants were seated on the deck overlooking the sea, waiting for the bus. They all told me it was a waste of time and that after four days, the glasses would be impossible to find. I dove into the forty-five degree water. It took my breath, but I swam down about twelve feet and there they were. My glasses half buried in the sand. I picked them up and triumphantly broke the surface of the water, holding them high over my head. The participants thought I had staged the whole thing to teach them a lesson about optimism and creating outcomes.

Did managing my emotions and staying optimistic affect the outcome of this situation? I'm sure that it did. By staying focused on the desired outcome despite what logic and common sense told me, the outcome was a positive one. I believe that I actually created that reality and affected that outcome by what I chose to think and feel. Imagine the power of this in your day-to-day encounters with life's challenging situations.

The latest neuroscience bears this phenomenon out. The way we view reality is based on emotional responses, no matter how objective we think we are being. That is the reason that "eyewitness" testimony can be very unreliable. If five witnesses experience the same event, you will likely get five different stories. Think of the consequences of this reality on a construction project. Think of the number of realities that must be reconciled in order to bring a project to a successful conclusion.

Let me repeat this. Our brains are hardwired for emotion. We can't escape it. The limbic system, or the primitive, emotional center of our brain, is working all of the time. There is an interesting case study in the book, *Emotional Intelligence*, by Daniel Goleman, a leader in this field. He tells us about Elliot, a successful lawyer, whose brain was damaged during an operation. The area that was damaged was the part of the brain that links the emotional part to the thinking part. Although he was cognitively intelligent, because he could not call upon the emotional part of his brain, he functioned more like a computer.

As a result, his life fell apart. "He could no longer hold a job. His wife left him. Squandering his savings on fruitless investments, he was reduced to living in a spare bedroom in his brother's home." Without this emotional link, the thinking brain could no longer assign values to the situations that arose. According to Goleman, "Every option was neutral".

Emotions also connect us. We have mirror neurons in our brains. These neurons mirror the emotions of the person sitting across from us. Try this. On a project or in the office, put a neutral look on your face and walk around. Note everyone's reaction to you. Now walk around with a smile on your face and connection in your heart and see if people react differently. Emotions are contagious. I don't mean anthropologically or anecdotally or socially. It's actually true from a physiological standpoint. Your emotional states cause mirror neurons to light up in the people around you, affecting them in a physical way! Imagine the power of that! Also, imagine the affect that you have on others when you are having a bad day. We are connected to each other in a very profound way. One Neuroscientist put it this way: "We are only separated by our skins."

Not only that, emotions create energy in the form of electromagnetic fields that can be felt several feet away from the body. That energy affects outcomes whether you are aware of it or not. Have you ever walked into a room and before you could process anything you immediately thought that the tension was so thick you could cut it with a knife? This is that emotional energy you are picking up on.

At the beginning of our first Total Leadership Program, we demonstrated this phenomenon. We sent Jonelle, our Executive Assistant, out of the room and told the participants that when I gave them the thumbs up, they were to think positive thoughts about Jonelle. When I gave them the thumbs down, they were to think negative thoughts about her.

She came back in, and we blindfolded her so she could not pick up on body language or facial cues. We sat her down and we performed kinesiology (muscle testing) on her. Basically, Jonelle held her arm out and tried to resist when Dr. Robbins, our resident kinesiologist, pushed it down. If she stayed strong, it meant that whatever she was experiencing was beneficial to her. If she went weak, it meant that whatever she was experiencing was detrimental to her. I started with thumbs up. She received positive thoughts from the group. She went strong. Then I did thumbs down. She received negative thoughts from the group. She went weak. I did thumbs up again. She went strong. After this, we heard someone from the audience say, "That's bulls#&*".

It was David, the COO of a glass installation company. David is a big, tough guy, a Marine, and a skeptical, no-nonsense person. His boss was kind enough to push him to the front of the room and said, "You try it." So, David came up in his camouflage ball cap, and we sat him down. Since he had seen the exercise, we decided to do a verbal version of it. Dr. Robbins tested him. He was quite strong, and David is a big guy. Keep in mind that Dr. Robbins is 5' 2" and weighs only 107 pounds. I told David all things positive, that he was a valued employee, that he was a great guy, great dad, great employee. His arm stayed strong. No matter how hard Dr. Robbins tried, she couldn't get his arm to go down.

Then, we went negative. I said, "David, you're a worthless piece of crap. I don't like you. I've never liked you. You're a horrible father. You're destroying your kid's lives." His arm went down easily. In fact, Dr. Robbins pushed it down with one finger. Then we went back to positive so as not to leave David with all of that negativity.

Here is the link to David's video:
https://bit.ly/2W7u6mG

David was a little shaken. We saw him later that evening and he told us, "There was no way in hell I was gonna let that little woman push my arm down." A few weeks later, we did an interview with David and asked him about his experience of starting off skeptical and then embracing this work. He replied, "I would encourage anyone to go without being made to go, because it will better you in more ways than you realize."

There is a device called the Emwave made by a company called Heartmath (heartmath.org). The Emwave monitors your Heart Rate Variability (HRV). This is an old technology that measures whether you are in a positive or negative emotional state. Heartmath calls this state "coherence". Participants can go back and forth between these states by thinking of something that made them upset or angry and then taking some deep breaths and thinking of things they are grateful and thankful for. It demonstrates how we can monitor and change our emotional states within a few seconds with some simple techniques and the right level of emotional self-awareness.

David had the typical alpha profile, but the Total Leadership Program changed his life and opened up opportunities for him. He was going through a rough time personally with a custody battle, long commutes, and children with health issues. He attributes the program with helping him to deal with these highly emotional and stressful issues and maintaining peak performance both mentally and physically. His wife's lawyer tried to get him to explode in front of the judge by baiting him during the custody hearing. He kept his cool and was awarded custody of his two boys. It also opened up opportunities for him at work. He is taking on more responsibility for the operations and leadership at his company.

The people who study emotional intelligence began by asking a very simple, but profound question: What makes people successful? They tried to quantify it. They looked at IQ and other intelligence indicators. They looked at higher learning and technical training. Did success lie in having the best education? What about MBAs, PhDs and other postgraduate degrees? Did they give people the competitive edge to become more successful?

Of course, the other thing that we need to define is "success". We could come up with a thousand definitions. Is it based on social skills, financial success, peer approval, a level of happiness? For the purpose of this book, we will try to simplify things. Let's define success as being a top performer in your field.

So, who are the most successful people? The answer probably won't surprise you. It isn't the people with the highest IQs or the people with the highest levels of technical or academic ability. Many of the most successful people have average IQs and education levels. So if it isn't technical skill, higher education, or intellectual intelligence, what makes people successful?

All things being equal, the people who excel are the ones with higher levels of emotional intelligence. Not that technical ability is unimportant. It is important for success, especially in the AEC industry. But technical ability and experience can only take you so far. One construction leader called it "the price of entry", but once that technical knowledge is in place, emotional intelligence is vital for ongoing success. One program participant put it this way, "Relationships and impressions are just as important as bricks and mortar."

The following is a graphical representation of the emotional intelligence and knowledge axes.

High Emotional Intelligence	
Steady Performer Moderate to High Success May Hit Career Limit Great Relationships Moderate to High Happiness Medium to High Stress	High Performers High Success Good Work/Life Balance Low Stress Self Development Great Relationships
Low Knowledge (Education, Cognitive Learning/Tech Ability)	**High Knowledge** (Education, Cognitive Learning/Tech Ability)
Low Performers Inability to Maintain Relationships Inability to Maintain Jobs Unhappy High Stress Blames Others	Technically Trained PhD's, Researchers, Engineers Can't Deal with People Poor Relationships Medium to High Stress
Low Emotional Intelligence	

For the purposes of this book, we will use "construction manager" as a generic term to include anyone who is involved in managing the various parts of the design and construction process. These managers tend to have medium to high levels of specialized knowledge, but average to low emotional intelligence and even lower interpersonal skills.

Most construction folks tend to be in the highlighted box. The technically educated people in the construction industry such as architects, civil engineers, and building construction majors receive very little "people skills" training while in school. There are few courses on interpersonal relationships, communication, empathy, or teamwork. I have also investigated the curricula of several MBA programs, and most of those programs do not cover these areas in any depth. It is a fundamental flaw in our education system, especially for technical people.

Several schools are aware of this deficit and are taking decisive action. They understand that although they are providing an excellent technical education to their students, they are not properly preparing them for the real world, where relationships are a vital key to their success. I am now working with the Architectural Engineering Department at Penn State and the College of Architecture, Design, and Construction at Auburn University. They use this book as a textbook so that students will have a better chance for success. This can be a difficult sell to faculty members at these technical institutions, but they are starting to realize that technical knowledge will only get their graduates so far.

Parker J. Palmer, in his book, *The Courage to Teach*, puts it this way: "If we are to educate a new professional, we must take our students' emotional intelligence as seriously as we take their cognitive intelligence. We must do more than affirm and harness the power of emotions to animate both learning and leadership. If students are to learn and lead well, we must help them develop the skill of 'mining' their emotions for knowledge."

On the field side, those who come up through the field under a mentor with good people skills will have a greater tendency to use these skills. But if they came up under one of those "old school" managers, they may be using the old "kick ass and take names" style to their own detriment. Managers who focus on these non–technical skills and embrace emotional intelligence become better leaders. One program participant said, "Improving my emotional intelligence built up my self-confidence and optimism. I started to think and act a lot more using emotional intelligence. We have stressful situations in my business unit and this has helped me to take my company through the hard times."

These leaders have learned to tap into that very important part of themselves. They have discovered that they can measure and improve these "soft skills", change behaviors, and increase performance. They become more effective both personally and professionally. There are dozens of testimonials documenting improvements in leadership skills and project results. Emotional intelligence also dramatically improves relationships, which contribute to increased job satisfaction, lower turnover, and much more opportunities for winning work.

There are several instruments that measure emotional intelligence. One of the most widely used instruments for measuring emotional intelligence is the Emotional Quotient Inventory, or EQ-i® 2.0. "EQ" (Emotional Quotient) to represent emotional competence as opposed to IQ (Intellectual Quotient), which measures intellectual capacity. EQ is the number. EI stands for Emotional Intelligence.

The EQ-i® 2.0 is a validated, self-perception instrument that measures five composite scales and sixteen individual emotional competencies.

SELF-PERCEPTION COMPOSITE

Self-Regard is respecting oneself while understanding and accepting one's strengths and weaknesses. Self-regard is often associated with feelings of inner strength and self-confidence.

Self-Actualization is the willingness to persistently try to improve oneself and engage in the pursuit of personally relevant and meaningful objectives that lead to a rich and enjoyable life.

Emotional Self-Awareness includes recognizing and understanding one's own emotions. This includes the ability to differentiate between subtleties in one's own emotions while understanding the cause of these emotions and the impact they have on the thoughts and actions of oneself and others.

SELF EXPRESSION COMPOSITE

Emotional Expression is openly expressing one's feelings verbally and non-verbally.

Assertiveness involves communicating feelings, beliefs, and thoughts openly, and defending personal rights and values in a socially acceptable, non-offensive, and non-destructive manner.

Independence is the ability to be self-directed and free of emotional dependency on others. Decision-making, planning, and daily tasks are completed autonomously.

INTERPERSONAL COMPOSITE

Interpersonal Relationships refers to the skill of developing and maintaining mutually satisfying relationships that are characterized by trust and compassion.

Empathy is recognizing, understanding, and appreciating how other people feel. Empathy involves being able to articulate your understanding of another's perspective and behaving in a way that respects other's feelings. Don't confuse empathy with sympathy. Empathy means that you understand and appreciate the other person's feelings. Sympathy means you feel sorry for the other person.

Social Responsibility is willingly contributing to society, to one's social groups, and generally to the welfare of others. Social Responsibility involves acting responsibly, having social consciousness, and showing concern for the greater community.

DECISION MAKING COMPOSITE

Problem Solving is the ability to find solutions to problems in situations where emotions are involved. Problem solving includes the ability to understand how emotions impact decision making.

Reality Testing is the capacity to remain objective by seeing things as they really are. This capacity involves recognizing when emotions or personal bias can cause one to be less objective.

Impulse Control is the ability to resist or delay an impulse, drive, or temptation to act and involves avoiding rash behaviors and decision making.

STRESS MANAGEMENT COMPOSITE

Flexibility is adapting emotions, thoughts, and behaviors to unfamiliar, unpredictable, and dynamic circumstances or ideas.

Stress Tolerance involves coping with stressful or difficult situations and believing that one can manage or influence situations in a positive manner.

Optimism is an indicator of one's positive attitude and outlook on life. It involves remaining hopeful and resilient, despite occasional setbacks.

WELL-BEING INDICATOR

Happiness is the ability to feel satisfied with one's life, to enjoy oneself and others, and to have fun. This is more of an effect of other emotional competencies. Happiness levels are affected by self-actualization, interpersonal relationships, optimism, and self-regard.

When the EQ-i® 2.0 evaluation is taken, the results are compared against a normative group, or a large group of people who have taken the evaluation. The numerical results for each competency fall into a bell curve. Similar to an IQ test, 100 is the mean or average. Scores ranging from 90-110 are considered average or adequate emotional functioning. Scores higher or lower than this range can indicate that the respondent is above or below average.

By measuring these sixteen competencies and, more importantly, by comparing the relationships among them, you can determine problem areas to target for improvement. Thousands of people in the AEC industry have taken this evaluation and not one has said that the results were invalid. In fact, almost all of the people have agreed that the evaluation was quite accurate. The validity scales that are built into the evaluation bear this out as they are usually well within the normal range. I believe it is because of the technical participants' desire to be accurate. They want the results to reflect their behavior.

Occasionally, a respondent will tell us that they think some of their low scores, such as empathy or interpersonal relationship skills, are inaccurate. First of all, we point out that it is a self-perception evaluation. The computer spits out what you put in. We also point out that these scores are relative scores to the general population normative group. When this happens, we ask them to show the results to the people who know them well, such as their spouse or close friend or colleague. Each time they have returned and told us that these other people agree with their EQ-i® 2.0 results indicating that they probably do need to work on those particular skills.

The following is a graph of 50 Superintendents:

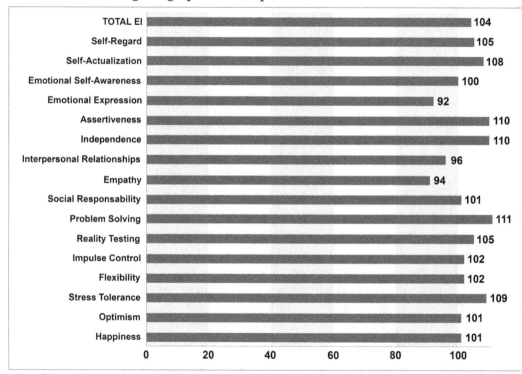

	Score
TOTAL EI	104
Self-Regard	105
Self-Actualization	108
Emotional Self-Awareness	100
Emotional Expression	92
Assertiveness	110
Independence	110
Interpersonal Relationships	96
Empathy	94
Social Responsability	101
Problem Solving	111
Reality Testing	105
Impulse Control	102
Flexibility	102
Stress Tolerance	109
Optimism	101
Happiness	101

Note the higher scores: Self-actualization (We love what we do!), assertiveness (above average), independence (above average), problem solving (above average), and stress tolerance (above average). Note the lower scores: emotional self-awareness, emotional expression, interpersonal relationships, and empathy (all at or below the mean or average). We also see the following patterns: alpha (high assertiveness, low empathy), control/ perfectionist (high problem solving and reality testing and low flexibility), frustration, impatience, anger (low impulse control, high assertiveness), and the lone wolf (high independence, low social responsibility). Note, when you see a five point or more delta between the highs and lows, that is significant. When you see 19 (assertiveness and empathy), that is very significant.

After seeing hundreds of these EI profiles for construction folks, this same pattern emerged. Although there were individual differences, every group with whom we worked had virtually the same EI profile. We have aggregated all of the scores from over 200 construction managers into a group EI profile for the AEC industry. These are all operations people. This group includes a dozen different companies and a wide cross section of people. The positions include assistant superintendents, superintendents, foremen, assistant project managers, project managers, senior project managers, subcontractor owners and employees, architects, engineers, building construction majors, business unit managers, estimators, sales people, production people, vice presidents, senior vice presidents, business developers, project executives, COOs, CEOs, and CFOs. There was a wide range of ages from the 20s to the 60s. The gender breakdown was 85% men and 15% women.

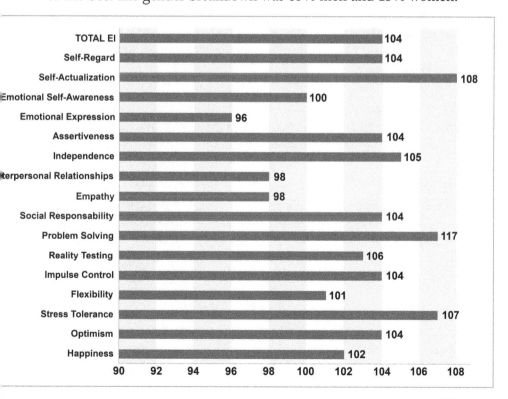

Take a look at the higher scores (self-actualization, assertiveness, independence, social responsibility, problem solving, impulse control, stress tolerance, and optimism). Take a look at the lower scores. The first thing that stands out is a relatively low score in emotional self-awareness (100), which is key for good emotional management. Emotional expression is always the lowest score for most groups (96). Think of the consequences of that with regard to communication. Other lower scores include interpersonal relationships (98) and empathy (98), which are both below the mean (100). Flexibility and happiness scores also tend to be relatively low.

Keep in mind that this is an average profile. Some of the participants scored quite high in interpersonal skills, making the average higher. We have worked with some participants whose interpersonal scores were in the 50s. Look at it this way, a group of over 200 folks who manage the construction process couldn't get emotional expression, empathy or interpersonal relationship skills to the mean. Low scores in the areas of emotional expression, emotional self-awareness, empathy, and interpersonal relationships are so pervasive, we call it "the quad". Many industry professionals we work with choose to develop one or more of these four competencies.

More importantly, with a differential of six points between assertiveness and empathy, most construction managers will be perceived as aggressive, independent, and capable, but many will come across as impulsive people who don't listen well, seldom ask for input from others, won't involve others in decision making processes, and are often blunt and undiplomatic. They also have a tendency toward the control/perfectionist profile (high problem solving and reality testing along with low flexibility). This group has a need for control and getting things "right". They have a hard time delegating and a tendency to micromanage.

This group also tends to have high stress tolerance and low impulse control. This is a chaos profile based on a reactive management style, which is inherent in the industry. Most managers go from crisis to crisis. Due to this crisis management style, they usually spend little time developing themselves or mentoring subordinates. Although people with this profile can handle a lot of stress, we have found that many exhibit physical symptoms of stress like fatigue, difficulty sleeping, pain, stomach problems, headaches, and irritability.

Also, note that without the strong interpersonal skills to balance competencies like assertiveness, independence, and self-regard, these strengths can become weaknesses. Someone with high assertiveness can become aggressive, someone with high independence can become a loner who doesn't interact with others, and someone with high self-regard can become arrogant.

We took this data and sliced it several different ways with some very interesting results.

Here is male (265) versus female (64) scores:

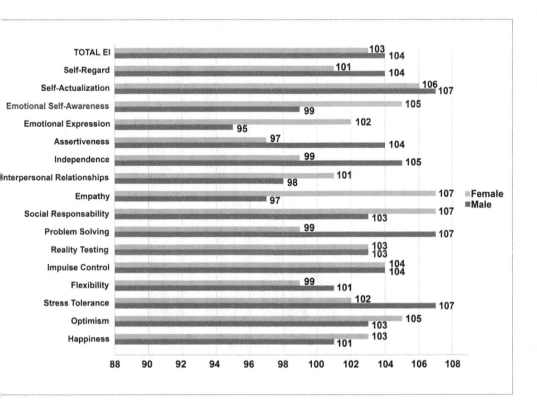

Note the highs for men: self-regard, self-actualization, assertiveness, independence, problem solving and stress tolerance. Lows are emotional self-awareness, emotional expression, interpersonal relationships, and empathy.

Note the opposite for the women: Highs are emotional self-awareness, emotional expression, interpersonal relationships, empathy, social responsibility, and optimism. Lows are assertiveness, independence, problem solving, flexibility.

This is strictly a graph based on gender. Many of the females in this graph are in support roles and are not managing projects.

With the industry gravitating toward more collaborative project delivery methods, companies who recruit and advance more women will be much more successful. As a group, they simply have better emotional competencies for collaboration.

Here is a graph showing differences by age:

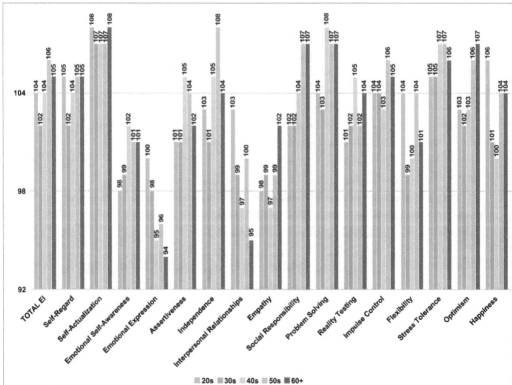

Note that total EI generally increases with age, but declines from age 50 to 60. The only exception are people in their 30s. They have the lowest in total EI and several other areas. There is no data behind this, but I know personally that my 30s was the worst decade of my life.

Also note that emotional self-awareness, emotional expression, empathy, social responsibility, impulse control, optimism and happiness generally increase with age. The exception to this is people in their 20s. They were the happiest of any age group. Assertiveness, independence, social responsibility, problem solving, and stress tolerance trend up, then down after 40 to 50. People in their 50s had the highest independence. Note that people in their 20s had the highest interpersonal relationship scores and it generally decreases with age. People in their 20s and 50s were the most flexible. This age graph can tell us a lot about the generations, their strengths, and how we can all learn to interact in a more positive way.

Here is a graph of 19 estimators:

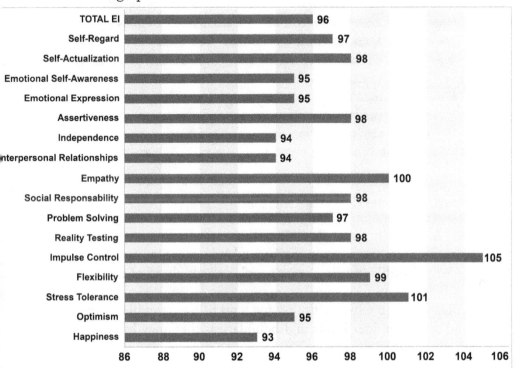

Note the high empathy, impulse control and stress tolerance, and lower scores of emotional self-awareness, emotional expression, independence, interpersonal relationship skills, problem solving, flexibility, optimism, and happiness. This profile suits estimators quite well. They tend to not be as social. There are many introverts, and they tend to be methodical and careful. Can you imagine an estimator with low impulse control, high optimism, and high flexibility? The estimates would likely not be as accurate.

Here is a graph of administrative people (12, all women):

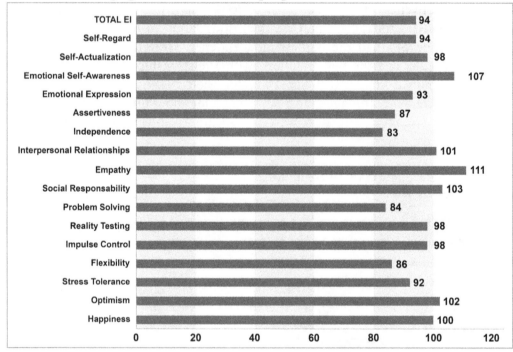

Note the high emotional self-awareness, interpersonal relationship skills, empathy, social responsibility, optimism and happiness and relatively lower emotional expression, assertiveness, independence, problem solving, and flexibility. This serves administrative folks well. They are there to support others and generally have the "self-sacrifice" profile (putting other people's needs ahead of your own).

Folks with the self-sacrifice profile tend to have trouble saying no and setting proper limits and boundaries. They may have trouble negotiating and firmly stating their beliefs. We have also found that self-sacrificers tend to be carboholics or sugarholics. They tend to eat a lot of carbs and sugar. We have located some studies that verify why this is true. When self-sacrificers help others, their brain generates a dopamine response and they feel good. When they are not helping others, sugar gives them the same response.

This profile is less common in construction managers, but more common for administrative and support positions. It would be very beneficial to know about this profile prior to hiring because this can be problematic for supervisory positions. We've all seen those poor souls who want to be liked and who just can't seem to stand up for themselves. By working on their assertiveness, independence, and self-regard, they can become much more effective.

Low self-actualization along with low happiness and optimism in a middle-aged person may indicate the proverbial mid-life crisis, which could affect productivity at work. Many participants with this profile admit that they are questioning their direction in life and the roles that they have, and they are not satisfied with where they are. If we can identify this situation early, help them to clearly define their roles and direction, we can make positive changes before they leave the company and buy that Harley motorcycle or leave the country to backpack across Europe.

This same profile is typical for new parents, especially when the score for social responsibility is also low. You've seen the new father, bleary-eyed, and exhausted for the first few months of the baby's life. This certainly affects his productivity at work. Both of these issues can be addressed by working on a clear direction for the employee's life and career and letting them know that this is just a transitory period in their lives.

If we see low self-actualization, stress tolerance, interpersonal relationships, self-regard, optimism, and happiness, this is a burnout profile. Stress and burnout are huge issues in the industry, and the cost is high in both business and human terms. The statistics on the increase in stress and burnout are alarming. You see these people all of the time in the industry. They are overweight and out of shape, with poor eating habits and dysfunctional lifestyles. They feel trapped and are caught in the downward spiral to poor health. They work too much, eat poorly, and don't exercise, which makes them less efficient mentally and physically. Then, they have to work even more and have even less energy left for exercise. This usually goes on until there is a health crisis such as a heart attack, auto-immune disease, or stress-related illness.

Accurate evaluation and early identification of stress and burnout along with lifestyle adjustments, proper nutrition, exercise, and proper stress management can prevent problems such as absenteeism, low productivity, and stress-related illnesses.

High assertiveness, low impulse control, and low flexibility may indicate a problem with anger management or other impulsive behavior. You've seen the guy who storms into the jobsite trailer, yelling and swearing and throwing his hard hat. It's not a pretty sight. In addition, nutrition can play a vital role in this dynamic. The first question I ask someone with an anger problem is, "What did you eat for breakfast?" Invariably, the tell me they didn't eat breakfast and when they reach the jobsite trailer, they grab a donut and a caffeine charged, sugar filled energy drink and go to work. The problem with that is that in an hour or so, their blood sugar will plummet and they will have the tendency to bite someone's head off. By working on these fundamental emotional competencies and their nutrition, managers are better able to control angry outbursts and work toward a fundamental change in behavior. This makes them much more effective in their dealings with project stakeholders.

Another pairing of competencies that indicates a particular behavior: high flexibility and low impulse control. We call this "chases shiny objects". These are people who are a little on the ADHD side, starting many things but rarely finishing them. They tend to float from task to task and have poor time management skills. They also tend to be Smartphone addicts. They can't resist checking their emails constantly.

For the AEC industry, there are several advantages to focusing on emotional intelligence as a way to develop people and solve industry problems:

1. With collaborative project delivery becoming the norm, many companies realize the importance of "soft skills" and invest in the training of these skills, but rarely know if the training has been effective. This is a way to measure and improve these critical people skills to produce permanent, fundamental changes in behavior.

2. Emotional intelligence may answer previously unanswered questions for individuals in your company. Employees may already know that they have difficulty with relationships or anger management problems. They may have been told during their review process that they need to "work on their people skills" or "be nicer to people". The problem is that they may not be able to pinpoint exactly how to do that. But once they take the EQ-i® 2.0 evaluation and see high assertiveness and low empathy which is likely the root cause of this issue, they are able to focus on these specific areas to create fundamental behavioral change.

3. Owners, Architects, Engineers, and Contractors like numbers. As construction people, we are obsessed with them – tolerances, schedules, budgets, manpower, productivity numbers, etc. Most construction folks are not shy about sharing their scores. They boast of high scores and sheepishly share their low scores (usually in the interpersonal skills) and vow that they will increase them. People in the industry are much more likely to embrace this work because it produces tangible results that can be measured and improved.

In fact, practitioners who work with Fortune 500 companies wonder why the results are so good with our programs. Part of the reason is that the people in the AEC industry are results driven. Once they see the value of this work, they attack it like they attack a tough project. They do the work necessary to create behavioral change. And these changes show up as statistically significant increases in their EQ-i® 2.0 scores.

Take a look at the following before and after graph for construction managers:

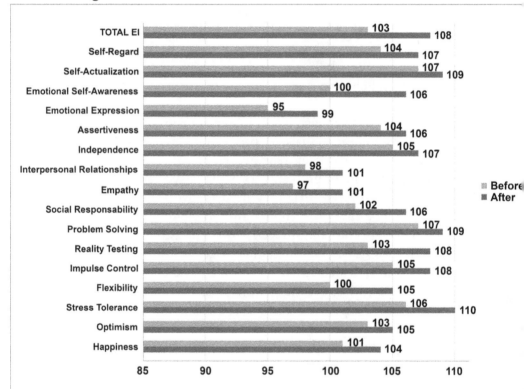

Note that total EI, reality testing and flexibility increased by a statistically significant 5 points and emotional self-awareness increased by 6 points. Also note the competencies that approached statistical significance of four points (emotional expression, empathy, social responsibility, and stress tolerance.)

The reason there weren't even higher increases is that with a larger group who are working on various competencies, the increases and decreases tend to cancel each other out.

Emotional intelligence is imperative for effective performance, especially with the shift toward more collaborative project delivery methods. If we evaluate our employees' emotional competencies, identify their developmental needs, and help them to work on these areas, they will improve these skills, increase their effectiveness, and eventually contribute more to the bottom line through highly successful projects.

Chapter 2

EMOTIONAL INTELLIGENCE, PROJECT SUCCESS, AND THE BOTTOM LINE

"People work for people, not companies. A worker's regard for his supervisor will affect his opinion of his employer. Production is related to attitude, so much so that an organization which disregards this human equation will not achieve as much as it could achieve".

Gerard R. Griffin

We talked in Chapter 1 about the "old school" construction manager. For those of us who have been in the construction industry for a while, we all know who the "old school" manager is. He's the one who kicks ass and takes names, the one who gets the job done. He doesn't take crap from anybody, punishes other project stakeholders, and holds their feet to the fire. He doesn't think twice about compromising safety if he thinks it will benefit him or his organization. If he is working on a hard-bid project, he fights for every single penny. He is willing to make others look bad so that his company can look good. It is his philosophy that since the next project will probably be exactly the same low-bid process, it is unnecessary to create and maintain good relationships. It is far more important to "win" at all costs.

But the face of construction is changing. The industry is becoming more of a service industry. We are getting away from the notion of delivering a building to an owner and walking away. We are seeing more design-build and negotiated projects, more integrated project delivery, more lean approaches, more team approaches beyond mere partnering agreements, more ongoing service contracts, and more repeat business. This "old school" guy is becoming a dinosaur.

The new construction manager not only needs high levels of assertiveness, self-regard, and independence, but it would benefit him to have balance in his emotional makeup. With this balance, he would be better able to deal with the myriad of people issues on any project. He would have strong empathy, communication, and relationship skills. He would be able to build teams and carry out a project plan with a sense of cooperation, constantly looking for outcomes that benefit everyone on the project. One of our program participants put it this way, "It is not what you know, but the way you present things. Leading and motivating is not just pointing and screaming."

Balfour Beatty is one of the top contractors in the USA. According to John Tarpey, a top leader at Balfour Beatty, there are four basic areas of product delivery for the AEC industry: schedule, budget, quality, and relationships. Most contractors are fairly adept at the first three, but it is the last area, the area of relationships, where many contractors fail. What will a project team remember a year after a project is complete? That the project was built on time, within a budget, with reasonable quality, or the relationships?

The industry continues to shift, creating a need for a new set of skills. Let's take a closer look at some of these shifts:

Old Paradigm	New Paradigm
Large labor pool	Competition for talent
Homogenous, male dominated labor pool	Multi-cultural labor pool with more females and minorities
Baby boomer workforce	Multi-generational workforce
Manage processes	Manage people
Low bid work	Negotiated work
Short, adversarial relationships	Long, satisfying relationships
Projects run from silos	Integrated project delivery system

Lack of client focus	Focus on client and his needs
Communication lacking	Communication focus
Decrease overhead	Increase performance
Safety a nuisance	Focus on safety
Environmental ignorance	Environmental focus
High Stress/burnout	Focus to reduce stress/burnout
Design/Bid/ Build	Collaborative Project Delivery
Low Tech/No Tech	Focus on Innovation and Technology
Productivity Stagnant	Productivity Focus Using Lean

This new paradigm requires a different set of skills than the old paradigm. The problem is that the typical emotional intelligence profile for construction folks is in direct contrast to the skills required for this shift. Let's revisit the typical AEC industry EI profile found in Chapter 1. In an industry where collaboration, good relationships, teamwork, flexibility, and communication are essential for success, the people who are attracted to this business generally have low emotional expression (unable to articulate feelings and connection), low self-awareness (lack of understanding self), high assertiveness (aggressiveness), high independence (not a team player), low empathy (lack of understanding of others), and low interpersonal relationship skills. The data is consistent and undeniable. Think about it. Many of the people in the AEC industry have this typical profile. No wonder it's such a difficult business!

Emotional intelligence is not some "touchy-feely" approach to management. It's not about group hugs, singing Kumbaya, and everyone getting along like robots. It's not about being nice or giving in. It's about positively affecting outcomes. As we said before, we are hardwired for emotion. It is integral to the way we think and interact with people. In short, emotional intelligence is all about physics and the latest neuroscience. It's about energy and how your brain works.

Understanding others helps us to be more effective. Peter, one of our participants put it this way, "I've learned that being able to understand what is motivating the other parties is essential for achieving your objectives." Another participant called this understanding "a definite competitive advantage". But with this typical AEC emotional intelligence profile, understanding others can be limited.

How many people can you think of in the AEC industry with this typical profile? How many employees has your company given up on because of their lack of people skills? Now there is hope for these people. By evaluating and improving their emotional intelligence, they will be able to thrive in this new paradigm. And for the folks who are already adept at these critical people skills, this work with emotional intelligence will take them to an entirely new level.

Most companies are not prepared for these industry shifts, nor do they know how to cope with them. The key to dealing with these shifts is in addressing the emotional intelligence needs of your employees and your company. In fact, it is critical for your future success. You must give your employees the proper tools, training, and encouragement to survive in this changing climate in the AEC industry. You must pay attention to their emotional competencies, evaluate them, identify developmental needs, and provide programs that will enhance their social competence. Without these skills, without the proper emotional tools, managers will fail in this new work environment.

Companies who ignore these trends will have unsuccessful projects, lose work, lose employees, reduce their margins, and eventually go out of business. Companies who pay attention to this vital work will hire great people, help them with their emotional development, create lasting client and stakeholder relationships, and thrive in this new marketplace. Their projects will be more successful and they will, ultimately, add a great deal to their bottom line.

Industry Problems

"You can't win without being completely different. When everyone else says we're crazy, I say, 'Gee, we must really be onto something.'"

Larry Ellison, *Founder of Oracle*

"Innovation is more than a new method. It is a new view of the universe, as one of risk rather than of chance or of certainty. It is a new view of man's role in the universe; he creates order by taking risks. And this means that innovation, rather than being an assertion of human power, is an acceptance of human responsibility."

Peter Drucker

"You can't invent the transistor by trying to perfect the vacuum tube."

Sign at Bell Labs

Introduction:

We are now going to delve into some of the more pressing issues in the AEC industry, issues not limited to the AEC industry. I'm sure you will recognize that these are problems in many businesses, especially technical industries. We will focus on probable causes, potential solutions, and how they affect project success and bottom line results. The root cause of many industry problems is the typical AEC emotional intelligence profile. If we can address these areas and create fundamental change in our people, it will have a profound effect on the entire industry.

Chapter 3

SAFETY ISSUES

A nyone who has ever been on a project where there was a serious accident knows that horrible feeling in the pit of your stomach when the radio crackles with the news that someone has been badly injured or killed, and you hear the siren of an approaching ambulance in the distance. No matter how successful the project is, that sick feeling is the one thing that will always be remembered.

Safety is a huge issue. Not only is there a moral imperative to improve safety, but accidents and other safety issues cost the industry billions of dollars per year in high insurance costs, lawsuits, Occupational Health and Safety Administration (OSHA) fines, and image problems. We all know that construction is a hazardous occupation. In 2016, according to the Bureau of Labor Statistics, 937 workers were killed on the job in the USA. That's almost three deaths every single calendar day. The International Labour Organization, a UN Agency, estimates that 60,000 people are killed annually in the world of construction. That's one every 10 minutes, and is comparable to the number of soldiers and civilians killed in state-based wars. The costs for not working safely can be monumental both in financial and human terms.

The leading causes of death among construction workers are falls from elevations, being struck by objects, electrocution, and deaths by caught in/between. These are known as "the fatal four".

What is the problem? Do people want to work unsafely? If you ask them this question, their answer is a resounding "NO!" When you ask top managers if they want their people to work unsafely, they answer, "Of course not!" So what is the problem here? The present system to ensure project safety is a command and control approach where strict safety rules are implemented. If the rules are not followed, the offending employee is reprimanded or fired. This approach has been marginally successful, but because we have only focused on the objective side of safety, we have reached the limit of its success.

To achieve the next level of safety for our workers, we must take a look at other causes of why they don't work safely. In our estimation, there are several untapped areas that lead to unsafe behaviors including poor judgement, cognitive impairment, and emotional intelligence.

Poor Judgment:

Poor judgment is likely a contributing factor to workplace incidents. I've heard many folks say, "You can't fix stupid." No, you can't fix stupid. But you can fix ignorance through education. If you pay attention, you can mitigate the factors that cause poor judgment.

When we are stressed, our judgment is impaired. Stress causes the thinking brain to shut down, which negatively affects our judgment. You can educate your workers on how stress affects their ability to work safely. Teach them stress reduction techniques such as meditation, mindfulness, and deep breathing. Teach them to take short breaks often and recover from the constant stressors on a project.

Drugs (over-the-counter, prescription, and recreational such as alcohol and marijuana) can also affect judgment. Many of the warnings from these drugs include the provision "do not drive or operate machinery." Yet, we don't really pay attention to that warning and rarely educate our workers on how it affects them and their safety. Take a close look at the common drugs that workers use and talk about the side effects. Are you or others on your project taking drugs that affect judgment?

Many drugs including antihistamines, sleep aids, and stress reducers can cause foggy thinking and poor judgment. Drugs like caffeine that jack us up (think energy drinks) are only short term.

There is usually a crash after a time and this is when judgment may be affected. Encourage moderation in their consumption of substances that negatively affect judgment and discuss alternatives such as better lifestyle choices, stress reduction, and better nutrition.

Sleep deprivation affects judgment, and was a likely factor in some of the biggest disasters in recent history: the 1979 nuclear meltdown at Three Mile Island, the massive Exxon Valdez oil spill, and the 1986 nuclear meltdown at Chernobyl.

A very large percentage of the population has trouble sleeping. They either can't fall asleep or they wake up and can't go back to sleep. Lack of sleep can lead to all kinds of maladies including fatigue and exhaustion. If you have a sleep disorder, you may be a walking zombie during the day.

There is mounting research on sleep and performance and safety. From an ASCE Technical Paper by Ronald Powell and Alex Copping, *"Sleep deprivation contributes to fatigue, which can have a profound effect on an individual's wellbeing, work performance, and safety, with an increase in risk of accident of 9%."*

The answer for many with sleep issues is a drug like Ambien or Lunesta. These drugs are highly addictive and it is very hard to stop taking them once you get hooked. Other solutions include CPAP machines, which may be helpful and over the counter solutions like zzzQuil, Unisom, or melatonin. These may provide short term relief, but none of them address the underlying cause of sleep issues such as stress and weight. And how many people take no action when they can't sleep?

Cognitive Impairment:

One other area that we can address is cognitive impairment. When we are cognitively impaired, we make poor decisions and don't recognize hazards. This is a recipe for a safety disaster.

What we put in our bodies affects us in many ways. When we put foods in that have little nutrition, our bodies don't work as well as they could. Firstly, poor nutrition causes fatigue, which is not desirable for good safety. When workers are exhausted, they make mistakes. Mistakes can be fatal. Secondly, when we don't properly regulate our glucose levels, we are impaired. A brain that is starved for glucose doesn't think as clearly and doesn't solve problems as readily.

Hydration is very important as part of good nutrition. Poor hydration can cause headaches and fatigue. Be sure to instruct everyone to stay hydrated throughout the day and drink plenty of water.

Teach your workers about the consequences of poor nutrition and hydration and be sure to give them healthy alternatives. Provide healthy snacks on projects and in your offices.

Work with your break truck operators and let them know that you're educating your workers about nutrition and hydration. Ask for them to provide more nutritious foods such as salads, fruits and vegetables, and more nutritious drinks besides sodas, energy drinks, and coffee. If they don't comply, find a break truck that will. Food trucks are a big phenomenon now, and many have healthy choices.

Some of our workers use nicotine and caffeine regularly. They take sleep aids and other over the counter and prescription drugs to alleviate the physical symptoms of stress. These stressed out workers are constantly visiting the white first aid box on the project for pain relievers, acid blockers, and drugs to help with allergy symptoms. Some of these substances affect their ability to think and reason.

Alcohol and caffeine should be moderated. Too much alcohol the night before and you fight a hangover where your body is dehydrated. You may not eat properly because of nausea. Also, caffeine is a good short-term solution for fatigue, but it is like a whip on the nervous system and when the effects wear off, your body suffers and your mental processes slow.

As we covered in the judgment section, when you are stressed, your body is in a low-level fight/flight state. It is being flooded with adrenaline and cortisol (the stress hormone), your breathing becomes shallow, which reduces the oxygen to your brain, your blood flow goes to the extremities, and your thinking brain actually shuts down. These stressful states impair your cognition and ability to think and reason. You must teach your workers stress reduction techniques such as meditation, mindfulness, and deep breathing.

As we mentioned before, most of our workers offset these physical symptoms of stress by taking over the counter or prescription drugs. All drugs have side effects that can impair our cognitive function. In addition, alcohol, marijuana, and other recreational drugs can also impair our cognitive function. People who are stressed experience physical symptoms that lead them to take drugs to alleviate the symptoms. These drugs have side effects that can cause cognitive impairment. Here are a few examples:

- Headaches and other pains may reduce your ability to concentrate and increase fatigue. Opioid painkillers will exacerbate foggy thinking and fatigue. Over 100 people die of opioid overdoses per day. You do the math.

- Antidepressants can affect energy levels and cognitive processes.

- High blood pressure and the medication can cause dizziness and fatigue.

- Sleep medication may make you groggy in the morning impairing judgment and cognition.

Teach your workers about the consequences of nicotine, caffeine, and drugs and give them resources to help them moderate these substances or quit taking them entirely. Offer alternatives on site and help them to live a healthier lifestyle if they choose. You can start an initiative to help people quit tobacco products and caffeine. You can address the underlying causes of why people take the drugs they do (mainly stress), and teach them stress management techniques so that they don't need the drugs. You can create an informal wellness program incorporating all of these elements. Let everyone know that you care about them and their health and well-being.

Imagine a person who stayed out late drinking and partying and who didn't get enough sleep, who had a big fight with his spouse that morning because of his irresponsible ways. They are having trouble paying their bills and will likely have to file for bankruptcy. He is late for work, still a little hung over, angry and irritable. He skips breakfast, arrives at the project, eats a couple of donuts, drinks a couple of Red Bulls, pops a Benadryl because his nose is running, and then climbs up into the crane. This person is in a highly stressful state, and it will negatively affect his judgment. An hour or so later, he is probably so out of it, it is like he is in a coma. He is a safety incident waiting to happen.

Emotional Intelligence and Safety:

The last part of an effective safety program is a focus on the emotional side of safety. According to philosopher, Ken Wilbur, objective approaches such as rules, laws, and regulations, as effective as they are, will always hit a limit, a barrier. In order to break through this barrier, you must tap into the subjective side of safety, the primal side, the emotional side. Emotional responses are far more powerful than responses to rules and regulations. Once you tap into these emotional responses to safety, this objective barrier is breached and you will improve the effectiveness of your overall safety program.

A contractor had five elevator workers that were not working safely. They were not tying off as they should. The superintendent called them into the trailer and had a talk with them. He sent them home and told them to get a letter from their wives saying that it was okay for them to work unsafely. As soon as he had those letters in his hands, they could go back to work. The elevator guys were a little stunned, and sheepishly went home early. The next day, four of the wives visited the project, and the other one called. They told the superintendent that their husbands had a responsibility to their families to come home alive and unhurt each day, and if their husbands were not working safely to please call them, and they would straighten that situation out in very short order. This is a great use of emotional intelligence with regard to safety.

When you think about it, every person on every project has loved ones – a family, a spouse, a partner, a friend, a child, a brother, a sister, a mother, or a father. When you look at safety from this highly personal perspective and make the emotional connections, when you put it in those personal terms, safety becomes much more than rules and regulations. Specifically, social responsibility, interpersonal relationships, and empathy skills are the keys to a safer work environment. But it all starts with emotional self-awareness. When everyone is aware moment to moment of their surroundings and are able to discern when they are too tired or too stressed to work safely, then you take safety to a whole new level.

Bovis Lend Lease in Atlanta used this type of program with dramatic results. In the United States, insurance companies assign a modifier based on past safety performance. This modifier is called the EMR (Experience Modification Rate). This EMR determines what companies will pay for worker's compensation insurance. The more safely a company works, the lower their EMR. Let's use an example: Say you are buying $100,000 worth of insurance for a project. If your EMR is 1.0 (an EMR of 1.0 is the industry standard), you will pay $100,000 for that insurance. If your EMR is 1.5, you will pay $150,000 for the same insurance. If your EMR is 0.5, you will pay $50,000 for that insurance.

Using an emotionally intelligent approach to safety, Bovis Lend Lease reduced their EMR to 0.34, so they would pay only $34,000 for that insurance. Bovis Lend Lease is not only saving lives and reducing emotional turmoil, but they are saving money and improving their bottom line. Imagine if the entire industry used this approach. The potential cost savings would be staggering, but the potential to decrease human suffering due to death and disability would be even greater.

Let's look at how some other industry issues relate to safety. Communication and teamwork are vital to working safely. Poor communication and ineffective teamwork can contribute to poor safety practices.

And what about alpha males as it relates to safety? There was an article in the July/August 2008 Harvard Business Review called *Unmasking Manly Men* by Robin J. Ely and Debra Meyerson. The article focuses on how roughnecks and roustabouts on oil rigs improved their safety by softening their approach and focusing on the safety and well-being of the workers. According to Ely and Meyerson, "Over the fifteen-year period these changes in work practices, norms, perceptions, and behaviors were implemented company-wide. The company's accident rate declined by 84% while productivity (number of barrels produced), efficiency (cost per barrel), and reliability (production "up" time) increased beyond the industry's previous benchmark." We have to wonder if this approach was ignored on the Deepwater Horizon oil rig, the site of the worst oil disaster in the history of the industry.

They further state, "If men in the hyper-masculine environment of the oil rigs can let go of the macho ideal and improve their performance, then men in corporate America might be able to do likewise. Numerous studies have examined the cost of macho displays in contexts ranging from aeronautics to manufacturing to high tech to the law. They show that men's attempts to prove their masculinity interfere with the training of recruits, compromise decision quality, marginalize women workers, lead to civil and human rights violations, and alienate men from their health, feelings, and relationships with others. The price of men striving to demonstrate their masculinity is high, and both individuals and organizations pay for it."

The key to this approach to safety is the emotional intelligence of the people on the projects; therefore the typical construction worker profile must be addressed first. We must start with emotional self-awareness so that workers are more aware of their surroundings, their bodies, and their levels of stress and fatigue. Then we should increase empathy skills, relationship skills, and social responsibility. That will make these types of programs successful. If we address these core issues, identify them, and take steps to improve them, we can create fundamental change that will help to take safety to a new level.

When people actually make emotional connections and care about each other, they look out for each other and work safer naturally. And when people work more safely, companies will save millions by lowering insurance rates, reducing worker's compensation claims, decreasing wrongful death lawsuits, and increasing productivity.

PRIMAL SAFETY®: A GUT LEVEL APPROACH

We have developed a safety program called Primal Safety®. This unique program states that everyone has the basic human right to go home alive and free from injuries at the end of the day. But with that right comes the responsibility to watch out for each other, to care for each other enough to point out unsafe situations, and to take the necessary corrective actions.

Employees and project teams focus on emotional competencies such as emotional self-awareness, empathy, and interpersonal relationship skills. Key team members take the EQ-i® 2.0 and develop the areas that are required for a successful program. Employees and project teams form closer relationships with each other with a deliberate approach to relationship building. Employees and project teams learn about each other's lives outside of work. This is done both formally and informally through activities for the workers and their families. Family members and loved ones become part of the safety process. Employees and project teams develop a greater awareness of safety – not because of rules but because the workers will care enough about each other to keep each other safe.

Primal Safety® program specifics:

1. The purpose of this program is to enhance the safety program that you already have in place.

2. The project team and any other appropriate parties take the Emotional Quotient Inventory (EQ-i® 2.0). We also have a free EI test available in Appendix A: Resources. You can also download the test by visiting this link:

   www.brentdarnell.com/resources

   This measures their emotional self-awareness, empathy, social responsibility, and interpersonal relationships. Without this foundation, typical construction EI profiles will likely limit the effectiveness of this program.

   One of the highest competencies measured by the EQ-i® 2.0 for construction folks is independence. Most of the folks in the industry defy death daily, working in a dangerous environment. It's like NASCAR drivers or bullfighters. There is an element of danger in what they do, and they are not fearful of death. But with high levels of independence, most have the fear of being dependent on others. If you tell them to work safely or die, you may get a smile or shrug of a shoulder. But if you say to them, "If you don't work safely, your wife may be feeding you and wiping your bottom", they sit up and take notice.

3. The basic premise of the **Primal Safety**® program is that everyone in your company has a moral imperative to implement an effective safety program for all workers, including trade partners, affording every worker the basic human right to go home each day uninjured to their family and loved ones. This means ZERO TOLERANCE! No incident or unsafe situation, no matter how small or insignificant, is acceptable. This approach is similar to how Bill Bratton, the former New York police commissioner, cleaned up the city. It was called the "broken window" theory. When there was a broken window,

it was replaced. When graffiti showed up, it was removed the same day. There was zero tolerance of the smallest of infractions, because if minor infractions were not addressed, it led to larger infractions and more serious crimes.

4. All employees are encouraged to report any incidents, potential incident, or unsafe situation, no matter how small. Every report is acted upon. Blame is not assessed, violators are not punished, and reporters are thanked and encouraged. The process is as follows:

   a. Analyze why the hazardous situation exists.

   b. Correct the situation.

   c. Educate the violators as to the proper means and methods in the spirit of learning and improving.

   d. Communicate these reports to everyone in order to avoid this situation in the future.

5. As part of the safety orientation, all employees share their personal stories about how they have been affected by incidents.

6. All safety activities are tracked and recorded including incidents, avoided incidents, unsafe situations and behaviors, corrective actions, and communications. Everyone has access to this information, which is reinforced at all meetings.

7. There are numerous activities to reinforce these safety concepts. Some ideas:

   a. At meetings, where possible, everyone should say their name and what they think about any safety issues for that day. They should be asked probing questions as well. According to the book, *The Checklist Manifesto*, the simple act of saying your name and giving your input makes it much more likely that you will speak up when something isn't right. When people don't verbalize their name and give their input, they are far less likely to say anything, even if they perceive that something is wrong. If this is not possible for large meetings, break your safety meetings down to smaller groups. And don't forget to have interpreters if necessary.

b.   The toolbox safety meetings should be fun and informative. You should not only discuss best safety practices, rules, and regulations, but address the emotional side of safety as well. How about trying walking safety meetings and mini-safety meetings. Walk around in large or small groups and point out safety issues like housekeeping, working from heights, scaffold and ladder safety, barriers and handrails, personal protective equipment, and any other safety topics that you find to be relevant. Ask them for their input. Ask them what they see. Ask them to point out what is wrong. The Primal Safety Toolbox Safety Topics are in Appendix A. You can also download the Toolbox Safety Topics by visiting *www. brentdarnell.com/resources*.

c.   Each morning, the entire project team does five to ten minutes of calisthenics and warm-up exercises. This reinforces the team approach to safety and prevents accidents by getting the blood flowing, warming up joints, and waking the team up mentally. You may also use this session to highlight a safety issue for the day. According to a Swedish study on a construction project, morning warm-up exercises increased or maintained joint and muscle flexibility and muscle endurance for workers exposed to manual material handling and strenuous working positions. Over time, this will decrease the number of injuries and increase productivity.

d.   Safety milestones are celebrated with jobsite lunches and team activities. These celebrations are also an opportunity to enhance the spirit of the team and create closer relationships among the workers.

e.   There are social activities outside of work to encourage the workers to create closer relationships with each other.

These may include sports activities, team sports, and other social activities.

f. Celebrations of birthdays, anniversaries, births, and other life milestones are encouraged. These celebrations reinforce the human side and put a face on safety.

g. A focus on quitting smoking and other tobacco use, good nutrition, weight loss, sleep, stress reduction, and exercise is a great way to let them know that you care about them as human beings. When they start implementing these concepts, their cognitive abilities will be increased. They will think more clearly, solve problems more readily, and work more safely.

h. Any way to remind them is beneficial. Everyone could wear reminder bands or stickers. Or everyone could wear pedometers if you started a walking or biggest loser contest on site.

8. There are family/social activities that reinforce safety. Some ideas:

a. All of the children of the workers make safety posters encouraging their parents to come home safely to them each day. The posters are laminated and placed throughout the project. There is a **Primal Safety**® Coloring Book for all of the workers' children. The book starts out with a child's entire family going off to work on a construction site. Then it shows how his family stays safe all day long by tying off, using personal protective equipment, keeping the site clean, and working together. There are also a couple of "what's wrong with this picture" pages that will create dialogue about unsafe conditions. In addition, there are Primal Safety Toolbox Safety Topics at the back of the book as well as in Appendix A: Resources. You can also download the Toolbox Safety Topics by visiting _www.brentdarnell. com/resources_.

You can order the Primal Safety Coloring Book from my website (*www.brentdarnell.com*). All profits from The Primal Safety Coloring Book go to a foundation that helps with suicide prevention in the construction industry. Our industry (construction/extraction) has the highest suicide rate of any industry with 53 per 100,000. For more information and resources, go to preventconstructionsuicide.com.

b. Put the photos of family members on hardhats along with their names. This will be a constant reminder of their loved ones and also create better relationships because everyone will be able to see your family and get to know them.

c. There are family days so that family members can visit the workplace and see demonstrations of the safety equipment that keeps their loved ones safe.

d. There are family social days such as picnics and parties. Every employee has someone who cares about his or her safety. Employees are not numbers. They are sons, daughters, fathers, mothers, brothers, and sisters. Find out which relationships matter the most for each employee.

e. Workers are encouraged to take their safety equipment home and show their families how this equipment protects them from getting hurt on the job.

f. Families are involved in the safety process. If there is a habitual violator, the family can be called in to help motivate that worker. This type of intervention has the potential to save lives.

g. Many projects now have webcams for security and also to check in on the project from remote locations. What if you started a campaign where you gave the families the web address so that they could look in on their loved ones while they were working? You could post signs that say, "Work safely. Your family is watching you."

THE FUTURE OF SAFETY: Where do you go after you reach zero incidents?

For a moment, look to the future and see a vision where the AEC industry is not only a safe industry, but actually becomes restorative. Imagine people working in this industry for years and retiring not only free from disabilities, but healthy and full of vigor. That is the next step in this process. Some say it is impossible to achieve. Some use the excuse that "this is a dangerous industry". Although there is no doubt that the work is tough and dangerous, we firmly believe that we can reach that level of health and safety through this emotionally intelligent approach and a true focus on people and their health and well-being. This will also address our poor industry image and workforce development issues. When we create this type of caring environment, people will flock to the industry.

Chapter 4

STRESS, BURNOUT AND LIFE BALANCE ISSUES

The AEC industry has always been a stressful industry. There doesn't seem to be any respite. During the great recession, the stress was associated with a lack of work and financial pressures. In better times, the stress is associated with too much work and stretching resources beyond their capacity. According to the CDC and the National Institute of Occupational Safety and Health's latest report:

- 40% of workers reported their job was very or extremely stressful;

- 25% view their jobs as the number one stressor in their lives;

- Three fourths of employees believe that workers have more on-the-job stress than a generation ago;

- 29% of workers felt quite a bit or extremely stressed at work;

- 26% of workers said they were "often or very often burned out or stressed by their work";

- Job stress is more strongly associated with health complaints than financial or family problems.

This is for general workplace stress. Can you imagine what these statistics are for the AEC industry? We can all see that stress and burnout in the AEC industry continue to rise. We are now experiencing worker shortages, so our workers are being asked to do more with less. The physical and mental demands are tremendous.

The World Health Organization estimates stress costs U.S. companies at least $300 billion a year through absenteeism, turnover and low productivity.

Some employees in the AEC industry work 60, 80, even 100-hour weeks, sometimes for extended periods of time. Take a look at some of the people who have been in the industry for a while. Some of them are overweight, look older than they are and appear beaten down and worn out. Frequently, these workers develop stress-related illnesses and auto-immune diseases such as heart disease (1 in 3 will die of this), high blood pressure, arthritis, and diabetes, which is fast becoming a major epidemic. The CDC predicts that by 2050, nearly one in three will have diabetes.

Too many of my friends in this industry have died at an early age mostly due to stress related illnesses. I have lost friends to heart attacks, strokes, cancer, diabetes, and alcohol and tobacco related illnesses. They ranged in age from 40 to 55. That is much too young to leave this earth. How many folks do you know that have died too soon from this stressful industry? How many do you know right now who are so stressed that you are worried about their health and well-being?

Workers use various Band-aid methods (caffeine, nicotine, over-the-counter and prescription drugs) to control the symptoms of stress such as headaches, stomach problems, allergies, pain, fatigue, decreased libido, anxiety, depression, high blood pressure, difficulty sleeping, and irritability. I could not find any reliable statistics, but improper work-life balance of most of the people in the industry certainly put a strain on relationships and relationship difficulties and divorce are all too common.

When I managed projects, I used to visit the shiny white first aid box with the big blue cross on the door a couple of times a day. I would reach in and remove the small, individual packets of sweet relief, popping aspirin for my daily stress headaches. After wolfing down my lunch consisting of a chili dog and French fries from the roach coach (the endearing term for the break truck), I would reach for a few antacids as a preemptive strike on my afternoon stomach problems. It was much easier to pop pills rather than address the underlying stressors, which were the cause of many of these physical symptoms.

Companies are beginning to wake up to this reality and address this issue. Using emotional intelligence, we can measure stress and burnout by measuring such traits as stress tolerance, self-actualization, interpersonal relationships, happiness, and optimism. The Total Leadership Program participants complete a physical survey that tells us how their body is working. With these two evaluations, we can determine if stress and burnout are problems and deal with them before they manifest themselves in the form of sickness, low productivity, absenteeism, and chronic disease.

According to Daniel Goleman, a leader in the emotional intelligence field, stress can be a killer, especially for those who have heart disease, the number one killer in this country. "Distressing feelings – sadness, frustration, anger, tension, intense anxiety (have you experienced these on a project?) double the risk that someone with heart disease may experience a dangerous decrease in blood flow to the heart within hours of having these feelings. Such a decrease can trigger a heart attack."

There is mounting evidence of this link between stress and general health. According to the World Health Organization, 80 to 90% of illnesses are either caused by or made worse by stress. They estimate that by 2020, the second leading cause of disabilities will be mental disease, including stress-related disorders. And with our industry (construction/extraction) having the highest suicide rate per the Centers for Disease Control, we better start paying attention.

In the United States, according to the *IMS Institute for Healthcare Informatics*, we will spend $610 billion annually on prescription drugs by 2021. In 2016, we filled 4.45 billion prescriptions. That's an average of 15 prescriptions per year for every man, woman, and child in the USA. The top drugs are analgesics (for pain), cholesterol medications, and antidepressants. According to the CDC, opioid prescriptions quadrupled from 1999 to 2014. Deaths from these drugs increased similarly during this time period.

According to the Center for Medicare and Medicaid Services, per capita spending on healthcare, the highest in the world, was

$10,348 in 2016 which is 31% higher than Switzerland, the next highest country for healthcare spending.

Some of these drugs, both over the counter and prescription, are taken to alleviate the symptoms of stress and stress-related illnesses. Recent studies also indicate that there may be a link between stress and obesity, a dire health issue in the United States, and prevalent among the AEC folks.

Did you know that the United States is the only industrialized nation on earth without a paid leave law? It's no coincidence that we are also the most stressed nation on earth. In the United States, we simply don't have enough downtime. Compared to other countries, our holidays and vacation days are ridiculously low.

Most workers in other countries have a minimum of five weeks of vacation and some have as many as twelve. Even the Chinese have a law requiring employers to give their employees a minimum of three weeks of paid vacation. This may sound ludicrous to all of us hardworking, take-no-prisoners Americans. I've known several construction folks who wear their lack of vacation as a badge of honor. They boast, "I haven't had a vacation in ten years!" But what is the cost? We are becoming a nation of stressed-out people with autoimmune maladies, hypertension, diabetes, cancer, and heart disease.

We must change the way we think about our time off or face these dire health consequences. Europeans we interviewed said that they need at least three weeks of vacation because during the first and last weeks, they are thinking about work. With three or more weeks of vacation, they are able to have at least one week of total decompression. We just can't get there with a mere two weeks per year. We usually take those two weeks in installments of three and four-day weekends. It just isn't enough. With these diminished vacation times, we very rarely reach a true state of decompression, especially when we take our phones and check our emails each day. According to a study in the book, *Work to Live: The Guide for*

Getting a Life by Joe Robinson, a yearly vacation was found to reduce the risk of heart attack by 30% in men and 50% in women.

What if companies started offering more vacation time, more flextime, and more ways for their employees to recover from stress? Even on projects, there are work processes that can be accomplished from anywhere. What if companies incorporated a ROWE (Results Oriented Work Environment) where employees were responsible for the results, but not the methods, location or time.

Could employees take a day per week or a day per month and accomplish these tasks from somewhere other than the jobsite? The costs would be minimal compared with the results. This would also address employees' need to set their own work schedules and be autonomous in how they accomplish their work.

Most people we interviewed said they would take a substantial cut in pay to be able to have more time off. By investing a little bit into their people, companies would have happier, less stressed, more loyal, more productive employees. Even at the craft level, if we were clever on how we managed projects, we could implement some of these ideas. Do you think there are craft workers who are "night owls" and would rather start later and work later? Would they be more productive? Could you manage the work to accommodate them?

Vacation is certainly one way to help deal with stress. But the day-to-day stress issues should be aggressively confronted by teaching managers to recognize symptoms of stress in their bodies, reduce these stressors, and build in recovery activities for renewal. This focus on stress reduction and recovery times allows them to have better performance mentally and physically. We teach managers how to handle their stress and create better life balance. One participant told us, "I have increased the balance in life, which has increased my efficiency at work."

One very effective way to renew the body is by doing yoga and meditation and practicing proper breathing and mindfulness techniques. We have many resources to support this work including a meditation CD, which is available on my online store at *www. brentdarnell.com*. I have been practicing yoga since 1978 and am a certified yoga instructor.

By practicing these simple techniques, employees are able to reduce stress and create better focus. This work with yoga and meditation is outside the comfort zones of most construction folks. I remember the first day of a management development program for a large, international contractor. It was very early in the morning, and we were starting with basic yoga and meditation. The room was empty except for some yoga mats. There was meditative music playing. I watched as these tough construction guys entered, walked back out to make sure it was the right room, then slowly came back in and sat down on their mats.

The thing that surprises me most about introducing yoga and meditation to the AEC industry is that almost half of the participants who have been exposed to yoga and meditation during our courses have continued these practices after the program has been completed. Even though some are reluctant to admit that they are actually doing yoga, they continue to practice it because of the tremendous benefits. Claus, a business unit president from Denmark said to me, "I think this yoga stuff is crap, but that deep breathing really helps me to reduce my stress."

Mariann, a controller from Sweden, was having trouble sleeping and sent me the following via email: "My job situation is extremely hectic again, and I have had some problems sleeping. Last night, however, I was able to calm down and relax using your meditation CD." Tom, a project manager from the United States put it this way, "Without question, the most helpful skill which I have implemented from my emotional intelligence training is how to better handle and reduce stress. By better controlling stress, I have seen positive results both at work and in my private life."

There is another benefit to yoga and meditation besides stress reduction. It actually enhances the emotional intelligence learning process. A recent study at the Indian Institute of Management in Bangalore found that yoga enhances emotional intelligence and improves managerial performance in organizations. Managers are better able to handle setbacks and they are less susceptible to stress. Because we are essentially rewiring the brain, creating new neural pathways, the yoga and meditation techniques help to create these new highways in the brain and speed up the behavioral shifts.

We also use visualization techniques to improve emotional competencies. Participants will visualize situations and outcomes that reinforce the behaviors that they want to achieve. For all of you doubters, ask any good golfer what they do prior to making a shot. The brain doesn't know the difference between visualizations and the real thing. The process is exactly the same, and it creates learning and behavioral change. We also use these visualization techniques to visualize project outcomes. It's very powerful.

Mindfulness is also a very powerful tool that we use. Jon Kabat Zinn teaches mindfulness techniques to executives. Mindfulness is simply being fully in the moment, without judgment, not dwelling on the past or worrying about the future. Clinical studies have shown that these techniques reduce cortisol, the stress hormone, and increase DHEA, the youth hormone. It increases focus and makes you more efficient.

And if you can't practice mindfulness all of the time, at least you can practice it during meals. Most of us wolf our food down or work during lunch. The average time to eat lunch for most kids is around seven and a half minutes. I encourage you to take at least thirty minutes for lunch and be fully present during your meal. Enjoy the tastes, enjoy how the food looks and smells and chew your food thoroughly. You not only enjoy your food more, you will likely eat less. It takes twenty minutes for your stomach to tell your brain that it is full. When you wolf down your food in ten minutes, your stomach still feels hungry and you have a tendency to overeat.

The more we study the brain, the more we see the connection between the mind and body. When we reduce stress, we reduce cortisol, a hormone that is secreted during the "fight or flight" response. Cortisol shuts down the thinking brain because when you are being chased by a lion, it is not in your best interest to over-analyze the situation. Without this hormone rush, we are able to think more clearly and solve problems more readily. We are able to be in a concept called "flow", where body and mind are in harmony with each other and both work as efficiently as possible. This results in fewer sick days and more stamina. Participants also report that they aren't exhausted at the end of the day.

Study after study confirms what we already know to be true. If we are sharp mentally, we function better physically and vice versa. Reducing stress through meditation has also been shown to increase the immune response and improve the body's healing process. But it goes beyond even that. Harvard Medical School is now studying meditation and the relaxation response and how it affects the body. What they have found is that regular meditation (you can call it prayer time, pondering time, me time, or reflection time) actually changes the expression of genes. It lengthens the telomeres. Shrinking telomeres are associated with aging and disease. Genes which previously may have expressed in the form of disease may not express when you practice regular meditation.

There is also a performance aspect to meditation. On their trip to decisively winning the 2013 season Super Bowl, the Seattle Seahawks practiced regular meditation and visualization. This helped with their stress levels and increased performance. They actually visualized themselves playing at a high level and winning that game.

Yoga and meditation certainly aren't for everyone, but we encourage participants to find "their" yoga. For some it is a sport such as golf, hunting, fishing, sailing, or some kind of hobby or recreational pursuit. It may be music or exercise or spending time with their family. It may be taking a mindful lunch daily or going for a walk.

Whatever your belief system and comfort level, you can apply these simple, but powerful techniques.

On one project we had laugh time. Every day from 3:00 to 3:15, we gathered in the trailer to laugh. Sometimes we told jokes. Sometimes we just laughed. It became this spontaneous thing that relieved tension and helped us to be more productive. This message of laughter has caught on in a big way. Laugh clubs are being formed all over the world. In fact, Glaxo and Volvo have organized laugh clubs in their organizations because of the positive benefits. No matter what you decide to do, the important thing is building in that reflection time and downtime each day where work is no longer the focus.

Companies are starting to realize the importance of addressing these health issues for their workers not only to make them more productive, but also to curb high healthcare costs. In an ENR article titled, "Wellness Program Cures Rising Health Care Costs", Cianbro Corporation, a large heavy civil and industrial contractor, addressed rising healthcare costs head-on. In 2001, they paid $11.5 million in healthcare costs, but these costs were projected to reach $20 million by 2004. So, in 2001, they started a voluntary wellness program for their employees. They reduced the percentage of smokers from 46% to 20%. 34% of their employees are exercising on a regular basis, and there has been a 20% reduction in hypertension and a 25% reduction in high cholesterol. Since 2001, instead of almost doubling, their healthcare costs have remained flat. In 2014, Cianbro not only reports that their employees and spouses have better quality of life, but they estimate that the company saved $2.4 million because of their wellness initiatives. This money goes straight to the bottom line.

The following participant came to us in total burnout. He was in a highly stressful work situation. He said he had no personal life. There was just enough time to go home, eat, and go to bed. He was overweight and smoking two packs of cigarettes per day. On his project, they were working a lot of long hours and there were a lot of unhappy people. His initial reaction to the program was negative. He didn't think the course would help him, and he had a difficult job to complete. Take a look at his before and after EQi:

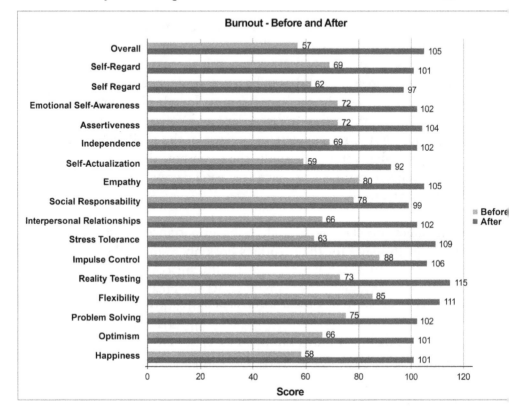

Burnout - Before and After

Category	Before	After
Overall	57	105
Self-Regard	69	101
Self Regard	62	97
Emotional Self-Awareness	72	102
Assertiveness	72	104
Independence	69	102
Self-Actualization	59	92
Empathy	80	105
Social Responsability	78	99
Interpersonal Relationships	66	102
Stress Tolerance	63	109
Impulse Control	88	106
Reality Testing	73	115
Flexibility	85	111
Problem Solving	75	102
Optimism	66	101
Happiness	58	101

Note, this is the older version of the EI test, which doesn't include emotional expression. We initially focused on his emotional self-awareness. Then, we shifted to self-actualization and created a plan for the future. We also worked on stress tolerance and increasing happiness. The change in this participant was amazing. A change in five points is statistically significant and indicates a shift in behavior. Take a look at the changes. This is a new human being. In his words: "Without the program I would have never known where I was and how to get me out of the hole I was in. Look at these techniques and no matter how ridiculous you may think they are, just try them and see what happens to you. Because it does work." He lost 20 pounds, quit smoking, and was much happier with his life and work. The project was a big success and led to a promotion for this participant.

We have added a peak performance component to our programs using a symptom survey to assess which systems of the body are under duress and address the issues of stress management, nutrition, sleep, and exercise. The amazing thing is that the results of this symptom survey correlate directly with the participant's EQ results.

One example: We worked with a 50-year-old Senior Superintendent who had low impulse control and high assertiveness, which indicated a frustration/anger profile. He was a volatile person. He was overweight and couldn't lose weight even though he ran twenty-five miles per week. He told us he felt like he had no discipline and that he just couldn't lose the weight. But discipline was not his issue. His symptom survey showed that he had problems with sugar handling. His body was not effectively converting his food to fuel. He needed sugar like an alcoholic needs a drink, and he ate sugar all day long.

This caused his blood sugar to spike and then plummet, increasing his volatility. By working on the physical part (reducing sugar intake and dietary choices through a weekly food log) and the emotional part (increasing impulse control as it relates to eating and anger), this superintendent made great progress. His sugar handling improved dramatically along with his impulse control. He was no longer volatile. He felt better and had more energy. He created better eating habits, continued his exercise, and lost thirty pounds. He began functioning at a higher level mentally, physically, and emotionally. The sad part of this story is that the company suspended our programs and without the annual check-in and follow up, this person gained much of that weight back.

This high level of stress and burnout relates to other problem areas. Stress decreases productivity. Pete, a project manager sent me the following: "One example of the benefit [of stress management] for me is that I used to take painkillers regularly for frequent stress–related headaches. Now I have learned to deal with the root cause of the headaches, and I rarely take painkillers unless I am really ill." By addressing the underlying cause of these headaches, Pete is now less stressed and more productive. Burnout also contributes to high turnover rates. Employees may leave their jobs in order to reduce their stress. Stressed workers also tend to make more mistakes, which can negatively affect safety, increase costs, diminish project results, and reduce the bottom line.

We have included our Body Battery Inventory, which will let you know how you are doing with regard to stress and recovery. It is in Appendix A: Resources. You can also download it with this link:

www.brentdarnell.com/resources

Chapter 5

COACHING ALPHA MALES

It always begins with a phone call. A top manager will call me and say, "I've got this guy. He's a great guy, very competent and knowledgeable. But he's pissing everybody off. No one wants to work with him or for him. A key client asked that he be removed from the project. Can you help him?" I've had dozens of these calls about these alpha males. I am continuously working with this group. In fact, that is the reason I was nominated for the ENR Top 25 Newsmaker Award in 2012 for "transforming alpha males into service focused leaders."

The industry is filled with these alpha males. They are strong, tough, highly motivated leaders who have a commanding presence and an aggressive style. These alpha males think they can do anything. My father, an alpha male in his younger days, tells the story of when he was a young carpenter. The layout engineer quit on a Friday afternoon and the superintendent asked my father if he could lay out the building. My father assured him that he could, then went home Friday to try and figure out how to lay out a building. He called a friend of his who brought over a transit and taught him how to use it over the weekend. In the end, he laid out the building without any difficulty.

These alpha males are extremely effective in certain areas, but according to a *Harvard Business Review* article titled "Coaching the Alpha Male" by Kate Ludeman and Eddie Erlandson, if these alpha males develop their interpersonal skills, they are even more effective. According to Ludeman and Erlanson, "Because [Alpha Males] believe that paying attention to feelings, even their own, detracts from getting the job done, they're surprisingly oblivious to the effect they have on others. They're judgmental of colleagues who can't control their emotions, yet often fail to notice how they vent their own anger and frustration. Or they dismiss their outbursts, arguing that the same rules shouldn't apply to the top dog."

They further state "the best way to capture the alpha male's attention is with data-copious, credible, consistent data." Our goal is to provide undeniable proof that his behavior (to which he is much attached) doesn't work nearly as well as he thinks it does." We use the EQ-i® 2.0, which gives the alpha male a graphical representation of his social functioning. If he is skeptical about the instrument, we can utilize the 360 EQ-i® 2.0, where the employees rate their own EQ while their subordinates, peers, supervisors, clients, family, and friends rate them as well. We do this to provide the "copious, credible, consistent data" that gets through to them. Once the alpha male sees this data, we have a better chance of convincing him that we can make him even more effective by improving his interpersonal skills. One participant put it this way, "Becoming aware of your own and other people's emotions makes you a powerful person."

If alpha males don't keep their assertiveness and self-regard in check, they can limit a company's financial success. As Daniel Goleman states, "A cranky and ruthless boss creates a toxic organization filled with negative underachievers who ignore opportunities; an inspirational, inclusive leader spawns acolytes for whom any challenge is surmountable. The final link in the chain is performance: profit or loss."

There was an alpha male named Ragnar in one of the programs I facilitated. During one of the moments where we share our thoughts about the program in front of the group, he said, "When I first started this program, I thought all of you were stupid. But the longer I am around you, the smarter you become." Ragnar, who was extremely resistant at first, was saying in his alpha male way that he was becoming smarter and more in tune with his emotional side. At the end of the program he declared, "[The program] has, against all my own odds, made me human."

In the book, Joe Torre's *Ground Rules for Winners*, Joe Torre, the former manager for the New York Yankees, discusses how he dealt with the large egos in Major League Baseball. He says it's not about a command and control attitude, but about knowing and caring for these world-class athletes in a personal way. If they know that you care about them and are looking out for them, they perform well. In his words, "To develop this level of knowledge about your team players, you need some insight into their personal and emotional qualities."

One of my favorite alpha male stories involves a superintendent in his mid-forties who was reluctant to accept the validity of this work. Although he scored high in assertiveness and self-regard and low on empathy and interpersonal relationships, he didn't see it as a problem. During our first session, he told me that he didn't really see a need to work on any of these competencies. He insisted that his job performance was excellent. And it was. I explained to him that I wasn't here to fix him because he wasn't broken. My job was to try and find ways to make him even more effective.

I asked him to share his EQ-i® 2.0 evaluation with people he trusted, and ask them if they thought he could benefit by embracing this work. They confirmed that he probably should work on his low scores. The more he thought about it, the more he was convinced that this would help his life and his career. So he made up his mind to give this emotional intelligence idea a try. Once he understood the concepts, he became highly committed to his personal development. He bought an iPod and downloaded dozens of audio books. He applied the learning each day, and brought his entire project team in on the process of helping him to improve.

After about six months, during one of our follow-up discussions, I asked him if others had noticed any behavioral shifts in him. He asked his superiors to let me know if they had noticed any changes. His supervisor sent me the following email. I have changed the participant's name to maintain anonymity:

"Bill has worked with me since 1998, and the recent changes are nothing less than remarkable. Since starting with our company, his ability and potential were obvious, but Bill resisted the necessary behavioral changes required to realize his potential. In the past, Bill struggled to maintain working relationships with individuals that did not display his level of commitment and was not understanding of those with lesser abilities. This created a lot of friction over the years as Bill's work ethic, determination, and ability are not easily matched.

He is starting a new project (one of the largest retail projects in the company's history) as lead superintendent, and I think this will be Bill's opportunity to prove to all that he is truly one of our very best." Another superior added, "I completely agree. Bill has really turned it around. I think he is a future star."

Gabriel was a 50-year-old Superintendent who was sent to us after being removed from a project due to poor relationships with the Owner and with his own team. He was devastated. He had the typical alpha profile, and we worked on emotional self-awareness and empathy. Take a look at his before and after graph:

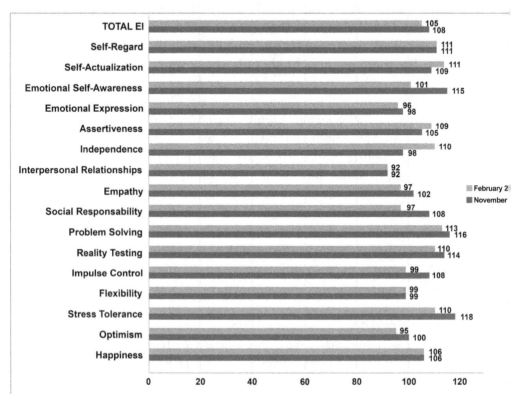

Note the increases in emotional self-awareness, empathy, social responsibility, and impulse control. Stress tolerance also went up dramatically. Note the decreases in assertiveness and independence. Empathy and assertiveness are oppositely correlated, so this makes sense. This shows a much more balanced profile and a person who is much more of a team player who is more aware of his emotions and able to handle stress better. In ten months, Gabriel went from being removed from a project to the Operations Manager for all of Mexico. During this process, he created such great relationships with a difficult client, that the client fired the construction management company and decided to work directly with Gabriel's company. He also reported that he was much better able to handle a difficult situation with a family member who had moved in with them.

We have dozens of these stories about these alpha males and how this work revitalized their careers. Before working on their emotional intelligence, they were successful, but it came at a cost to themselves and others. When we told them that other people saw their driving approach as negative they were shocked. They tell me that they care about those other people and the project so much that they push very hard. So hard, in fact, that the people being pushed get fed up with it.

Our approach is to tell them that we can help them to be even more successful with a lot less wear and tear on themselves. For the many alpha males in the AEC industry, this emotional intelligence work can make them even more effective by tempering their dominant attitudes and behaviors with great interpersonal skills and impulse control. Alpha males are all about performance and results. And this approach to create more balance in their EQi-2.0 profile makes them more approachable. They are able to better motivate others and make connections with people that create amazing results.

They will likely be resistant at first, as most construction managers and alpha males are, but once they see the benefits and become aware of the errors associated with their present leadership style, they doggedly pursue this work and become better leaders. They will also be able to more effectively deal with all of the project stakeholders and increase project success and bottom line results.

Chapter 6

INDUSTRY IMAGE, CUSTOMER SERVICE AND WORKFORCE DEVELOPMENT

Industry Image

As most of you well know, the AEC industry has a poor image. After performing my own informal survey asking many people about their experiences with contractors, their responses were invariably negative. Many contractors are viewed as unethical, untrustworthy, and difficult to deal with. I remember watching one of those Naked Gun movies. They lampooned just about everyone from law enforcement officials to politicians. When the villain was asked how he could do something so vicious, he replied, "It was easy my dear, don't forget I spent two years as a building contractor."

Careercast ranks the top 220 jobs each year based on several factors:

1. Work Environment (Physical and Emotional)
2. Income
3. Outlook (will this job be here in the future?)
4. Stress

The top-rated job is number one and the least desirable job is rated 220. Year after year, AEC industry jobs are rated at the very bottom.

The only AEC job ranked in the top 50 was Civil Engineer at 45. The sad fact is that construction industry jobs have been at the bottom of the list for years. The only jobs making it to the top 100 were Mechanical Engineer (57), Electrical Engineer (72), OSHA Inspector (79), Architectural Drafter (81). Most of the other AEC jobs ranked in the bottom 100 and eight jobs ranked in the bottom 50. Some jobs that most consider menial (janitor, funeral director, sewage plant operator, nuclear decontamination technician, and garbage collector) ranked higher than many construction jobs. It's no wonder that young people stay away in droves.

Here are the rankings:

45 Civil Engineer
57 Mechanical Engineer
72 Electrical Engineer
81 Architectural Draftsman
110 Plumber
113 Construction Manager
122 Surveyor
130 Building Inspector
131 Funeral Director
136 Janitor
156 Sewage Plant Operator
161 Equipment Operator
169 Garbage Collector
171 Nuclear Decontamination Technician
179 Glazier
183 Iron Worker
185 Architect
192 Carpenter
195 Sheet Metal Worker
198 Roofer tied with Welder
201 Mason

Industry professionals have continually tried to address this image issue with little success. Way back in 2004, Engineering News Record penned an article titled, "Industry Image Initiative May Be Dying". The editorial states that very little progress has been made to improve the industry image.

There are some very good new initiatives in conjunction with industry associations like the AGC that are quite promising. There are hands on museums for young builders and engineers where they actually use tools and build things. There is the ACE Mentoring Program. Home Depot and Lowe's have classes for children to encourage these future do-it-yourselfers. There is Dozer Day in Washington state that allows families to actually operate construction equipment. There is even a construction theme park called Diggerland, which features attractions that are modified heavy equipment that families can operate.

These are great initiatives, and will likely have some impact down the road, but what about now? With the recession all but behind us, this workforce development issue is staring us in the face. And we must address this industry image now.

So why is our industry image so poor? There are many factors. They include non-competitive wages and benefits (health insurance, paid vacations, sick days, and retirement programs) and poor working conditions. We must address those issues. But I believe that there is one issue that has not been addressed that could be addressed immediately. And that is the attitude of the people in the industry. This work with emotional intelligence can improve those attitudes dramatically.

From the age of fifteen, I worked every summer on various construction projects as a laborer, carpenter's helper, and layout engineer. I loved the work, but I didn't care for some of the people with whom I had to work. They were tough and aggressive. There was one foreman in particular who was downright scary to me. I was afraid to ask about anything for fear that I might appear stupid, and I never wanted to make a mistake. Think of the consequences of this attitude with regard to safety.

I remember a time when I stepped on a nail, but was so afraid to tell him, that I went home with a hole in my foot and a blood-soaked sock. Back when I was working summers, the business was tough. Developing a thick skin was a must for survival. There was very little training or orientation. The attitude was, "Throw them in the deep end. If they can't figure it out, we don't want them here."

It was like some arcane fraternity, and the initiation process was difficult. These construction people with specialized knowledge would send me after non-existent "board stretchers" and "sky hooks". One time, my boss sent me to fetch a "come-a-long". Well, I had no idea what a "come-a-long" was, but I wasn't about to tell him that. I went to the tool shed and tried to find something that looked like a "come-a-long". Somewhere in the back of my mind, I thought that this was another wild goose chase similar to the "board stretcher" I tried to find the previous week. I was certain that when I returned, everyone would laugh at me. Despite these fears, I pressed on and chose something. By some miraculous twist of fate, I chose the right thing. Now, when I look back at these experiences, I think to myself, "What a screwy business, where you are so afraid of being the butt of a joke that you won't ask when you don't know something."

One other incident sticks in my mind concerning the attitude of the people in the business back then. I was an engineering student at the Georgia Institute of Technology and was working during the summer of 1979 as a layout engineer. We had purchased a Leibherr tower crane, and they sent a German engineer to help with the assembly and setup. We had poured a test weight with hooks embedded in the concrete for the crane to lift. The engineer asked me to determine the weight of the block. I pulled out my trusty handheld calculator along with my handy book that told me the weight per volume for concrete. I punched in the calculation and proudly wrote the result on the top of the concrete block.

Since I fancied myself to be an engineer, I wanted to be really accurate and precise so I carried the number out to six decimal places. When the engineer saw it, he called everyone around and said, "Hey everybody. Look here. Look what the college boy did. He figured up the weight of this piece of concrete." He took out a large Magic Marker, brushed off some of the stray aggregate and dust from the top of the block and marked through all of the numbers after the decimal. "Hey, stupid college boy, when you're dealing with thousands of pounds, you don't need so many decimal places. Or didn't they teach you that in school?" He then brushed more of the dust off, laughed, and said, "That dust I brushed off just changed your number." It wasn't a motivating experience. We can do better.

Customer Service

Ask most owners. The perceived level of customer service in the industry can be quite low. Not long ago, the Vice President of a top five US contractor said to me, "I think the problem is that we just don't have enough empathy to understand and address the needs of our clients." Given the typical profile for most construction managers, this statement is undeniably true.

As a group, most of these managers have low empathy skills, which can prevent them from providing great customer service. If this fundamental lack of empathy is addressed, along with other interpersonal relationship skills, customer service can be significantly improved. One program participant put it this way, "My interpersonal interactions with customers, colleagues, and subordinates have improved by being able to establish a deeper communication."

I watched a video as the head of a large hospital addressed potential contractors for their upcoming building campaign. It was one of the best sessions I've ever seen that addresses this issue from an owner's perspective. The first thing she said was that every contractor there was excellent. She said that construction is an emotional process and that owners don't even know what they want. She assured the contractors that the hospital would be irrational. They would fail to listen. They would make mistakes. She further stated that it was the contractor's job to understand these emotional states and this irrational behavior and be able to guide them through this very difficult process and respond to all of their many personal and professional needs. Wow! Talk about a different set of skills to be able to deliver great customer service!

I had a participant, I'll call him John, a quality control person who was having some difficulty dealing with the representatives from the Corps of Engineers, who have a reputation for being very demanding clients. John scored very high in assertiveness and low in interpersonal relationships and impulse control. He told me that he really didn't like these Corps guys, and he tried to prove them wrong and punish them for their mistakes every chance he got. Most of the time, he just reacted to situations and relished the idea of making them look like fools. I asked him how that was working for him. He said that he felt like he was winning battles but losing the war.

I had to find something that would work for John, something that would enable him to give the Corps better customer service. As it turns out, John was a devout Catholic. I asked him to picture the Corps representatives with "EGR" stamped on their foreheads. He asked me what "EGR" stood for. I told him, "Extra Grace Required". I pointed out that this was his chance to give them a gift they may not even deserve. He really liked this idea of applying his religious beliefs and implemented it with great results.

As he put it, "When faced with a conflict or difference of opinion, I've been very conscientious of letting others speak their minds while concentrating on their positions and feelings. This approach has produced positive outcomes, and I feel that by continuing to use this approach in difficult situations, I will improve and become more successful in resolving conflicts." His relationship with the Corps improved and enabled him to more easily close out the project.

Another story comes to mind with regard to customer service. I received a call from a company that told me that they had an executive with the company, who was a very talented person. He was a typical alpha, hard charging and results driven. The company was told by several owners that they didn't want this executive on their projects. Although he had the best of intentions, the owners did not like him and their perceived level of customer service was very low. They saw him as a liability, not an asset.

The company told this executive that he had to make some changes or they may have to take some further action with him. He was enrolled in a class with some other folks in the company, and he has really turned things around. Now owners ask for him by name. His relationships are so strong with clients and potential clients that this company is now procuring work without bidding. They believe that he truly is there to take care of them and make their life easier.

One of the things you may be faced with during this emotional intelligence journey is the hard reality that you may have to fire some of your best people. Some of these high performers don't possess the people skills to be able to deliver these high levels of customer service. In fact, they may be harming your company by destroying relationships with clients, subordinates and other stakeholders. There is hope for these folks if they want to create these changes. But if they don't you may have to let them go.

How many customers is your company losing because of your employees' poor people skills?

It may not be enough to take your employees through "customer service" training. Given the typical construction managers' profiles, an eight-hour lecture stating a list of things to do to provide great customer service may not be effective since their lower empathy and interpersonal skills would prevent them from applying this information in a meaningful way.

Companies must pay attention. Poor customer service due to a lack of people skills may be deteriorating client relationships while you are reading this book. If you address these fundamental emotional competencies now, you can improve your customer service. And improved customer relations mean successful projects, satisfied clients, referrals, and repeat business, which has a direct impact on project results and your bottom line.

Workforce Development

There is no doubt that this "alpha" attitude has improved over the years, but there is still some work to do. It's no wonder that the numbers of young people coming into the industry are dwindling, especially in the trades. Because of these dwindling numbers, we had come to rely on immigrants to fill these positions. During the great recession, many immigrants fled, and they aren't likely to return. They no longer desire these positions. Without this influx of immigrants, and a targeted crackdown on illegal immigration, we do not have the work force to build projects.

There is also a shift in demographics. Baby boomers are beginning to reach retirement age, and there are smaller numbers of generation X and millennials to replace them. And what about generation I (the internet generation or generation next)? All industries will be competing for this shrinking talent pool. Consultants make a lot of money telling us about generalizations and stereotypes for each generation and how to overcome them.

They tell us that generation X and millennials are motivated by a different set of values than the baby boomers, that they are drastically different in their approaches to life and work. They create long lists of generalizations for each generation and give us guidelines to be able to deal with them effectively.

Take a look at the following quote (paraphrased): "We are more worthless than our fathers and we shall give the world a future generation even worse." When do you think this was spoken? I've had folks guess the 1950s, the 1970s. Give up? It was said by Horace in his Book III of Odes written around 20 BC.

This discussion about generations is nothing new. It's been going on for a long time. What is really different? It's communication and technology. But this isn't a generational issue. It's a people and communication issue. Even with differences in approaches to life and work, we are all human beings and are motivated by what makes us human. This is the beauty of emotional intelligence.

Some baby boomers are reluctant to make any adjustments to how the younger generations work. They believe that they are just lazy and don't have the same work ethic that they do. This is simply not true. Although I can think of one millennial who is really lazy. His name is Mark Zuckerberg, the founder of Facebook, and worth around $65 billion.

These young people are highly motivated and highly educated. They want to move up fast. They want to know what you know. If you throw these young folks into the deep end of the pool to sink or swim, if you ignore them and tell them to shut up and work hard, if you give them meaningless work so that they can "pay their dues" like you did, if you don't let them participate in important decision making processes, they will certainly leave.

Everyone needs more autonomy, purpose, and a clear career path with resources to attain the skills they need to succeed. One bonus item to provide for better retention: Make their life better. If you make their lives better, they will be less likely to leave you. Provide wellness resources, financial planning resources, and support for their personal lives.

These demographic and economic issues will be difficult to overcome, but there is one issue that contributes to this industry image problem that we can control. It is the attitudes of the people in the industry. What it boils down to is this human dimension. If we focus on leadership qualities like great interpersonal skills, we can greatly improve the industry image. These leaders must learn how to encourage workers and find what they are passionate about.

Diversity and Inclusion is also part of the workforce development issue. We must learn to be more inclusive and embrace diverse ways of thinking, diverse ideas, and promote diversity in our workforce. Some basics: Look at your company website and see if it expresses diversity. Move women and minorities up quickly and make sure the C suite is diverse so that younger folks coming in can have role models and be more inclined to stay. Give them specific career paths so that they know that top management is a definite option. Recruit from non-traditional sources and seek out folks who are traditionally different from your normal recruits.

We must teach our leaders to communicate well, to listen and truly care about the people who work for them no matter what their age or gender. This will go a long way toward fixing this poor image while sending the message that this is an industry where you will be respected and encouraged to thrive. If we can find ways to improve this industry image, we will tap into this future workforce, improving clients' trust, working relations, and the way we do business. This will have a direct, positive effect on project success and the bottom line.

The Three Rs of Workforce Development

Everyone is talking about the workforce development issue, but other than a few recruitment initiatives, little is being done. What if we had an integrated, systems thinking approach?

If we want to save the industry and be truly competitive and capture this future workforce, there are three things we must do:

1. Redesign. We must go back to the drawing board and take a hard look at how we design and build buildings and other projects. We lament that there is not enough skilled labor instead of designing projects where you don't need so much skilled labor. We need to take a look at 3D printers, prefabrication, modular fabrication, robotics, and other high tech and cutting-edge solutions. This re-examination will very likely help to save the industry.

    When I traveled to Sweden, I was surprised that they put almost all electrical wiring in trays, even higher voltage wiring. I asked them why they didn't run them in conduit. They said it is not needed. Let's create better designs and then provide the labor to accomplish whatever is required.

2. Recruit. We must start recruiting early and follow the examples of the ACE Mentoring Program (targeting high school kids) as well as other mentoring efforts. We must start contacting these future leaders of the industry, pass on our knowledge, nurture them, and instill our passion for the industry in them. We must focus more on women and minorities and welcome

them into this beautiful industry where we create something from nothing. This needs to happen on all levels of education. We must also work on improving our industry image, and we can do that by showing these young people our passion. What if every construction project in the country started a local outreach program to schools and gave tours to the students to show them all about the construction industry!

We must also utilize non-traditional recruiting sources and develop training programs for returning veterans, people who are experiencing homelessness, and people who are incarcerated. There is a large, untapped workforce out there, and we need to create the vehicles to bring them into the industry.

3. Retain. In order to retain these great people once they have committed themselves, we must offer them something more than a job. We must provide our workers (especially craft workers) healthcare and paid time off. We must provide the tools for their personal and professional development. We must take an interest in them as human beings, care about them and help them through their life's journey. We must invest in them, train them, and be there for them. If you were taken care of to that level, would you leave? We must show them the bigger picture of the industry and how wonderful it is to help educate our kids, heal our sick, house us in beautiful spaces, allow us to travel from place to place, and provide us entertainment and escapes that help us to relax from the burdens of this life. What a noble profession that is!

Chapter 7

EMOTIONAL INTELLIGENCE AND MARKETING

Are most of your project chases based on price alone? Have you cut your overhead and profit down to next to nothing and still find it hard to compete? Do you find it hard to differentiate your company in this highly commoditized market? Do you think that owners only look at price? If this is the case, then this chapter is vital for you and the future success of your company.

The first thing we must look at is how people make buying decisions. And although some contractors tell me that the buying decision is made on price alone, in many cases, this is simply not true. And if an owner does use a low bid process, it's usually due to legal or institutional requirements. Even this approach is starting to change because owners know that this design/bid/build approach oftentimes creates poor project outcomes.

At a recent Associated General Contractors national meeting, two large owners' representatives (Disney and MD Anderson Cancer Center) were asked how they chose contractors. The contractors in the audience had their tablets and pens at the ready. They were going to find the magic formula, that one thing that would differentiate them from the competition. Was it a fee below a certain percentage? Was it resume? Was it schedule compression? Innovation?

To everyone's shock and amazement, they both said that, "It was just a feeling we have during the interview process." They could tell which project teams would work well together and with them. They emphasized that if you are in that room for an interview, you were capable of building the project. It really comes down to those intangibles of relationship and emotional connection.

The latest neuroscience bears this out. Daniel Kahneman is a Nobel prize winning psychologist who studied why people buy stuff. And what he found out was a little shocking. Purchasing decisions, whether they are for products or services, are formed in our subconscious or System 1 mind. The System 2 mind is the cognitive part and has zero input into decision making.

There is another great book called *Habit: The 95% of Behavior That Marketers Ignore* by Neale Martin. It further reinforces this concept. And yet, what do we do when we present for a project? We focus on our resume, the experience of our project teams, the site logistics, the schedule, and the budget. We say that we will build the project on time, with good quality and safety. Blah, blah, blah. You and everyone else.

According to Martin, your customer is looking for shortcuts to good decisions. There are two basic ways that the brain approaches thinking and decision making: Martin calls them the habitual mind (System 1) and the executive mind (System 2). Take a look at the following:

Your response is from your habitual mind or subconscious. You don't have to think about it. It's automatic. You automatically react positively to a smiling baby.

Now try to solve this in your head: 578 X 634 =

You are now engaging your executive mind (System 2) or the prefrontal cortex. And it's hard. It takes effort. It takes energy. Your brain burns a lot of glucose trying to solve that equation. And as it turns out, the System 2 brain is very lazy. It is on a constant quest to conserve energy. You probably gave up pretty quickly with trying to solve that equation in your head. By the way, for all of you number nerds, the answer is 366,452.

On a personal level, think of mayonnaise. If you don't like mayonnaise, think of peanut butter. What is your brand? Is it Kraft, Hellman's, Dukes', Miracle Whip, Blue Plate? Skippy, Jif, Smuckers? Do you look at the price when you purchase it? If there was a mayonnaise or peanut butter beside your brand called Jerry's Mayonnaise or Jerry's Peanut Butter, and it was 50 cents cheaper, would you buy it? Of course not. That purchasing decision is based on emotion and memory. You probably grew up with that mayonnaise or peanut butter. You may remember a wonderful sandwich made with it. You have an emotional connection to that product.

Think of another example: Disney. Is Disney the cheapest place to go? Of course not. But the park is packed with people who have brought their children because of an emotional connection to Disney that was instilled in them as children.

Our mantra for companies who embrace this work with emotional intelligence and marketing is that you must create a positive emotional experience instead of just a transaction. So what kind of emotional experiences are you creating in your offices and on your projects right this very minute? What do people feel when they walk into your office or the jobsite trailer? What kind of emotional connections are you making with your outgoing messages? Most outgoing messages I listen to are pretty horrible. Some are just the number. I always redial those thinking that I have reached a wrong number. Is your outgoing message transactional or connecting?

I'm going to give you two scenarios. These are actual scenarios from companies that I visited. I want you to decide which company you would rather do business with:

Scenario 1: I walk into the office. It is a stark place with grey walls. The receptionist doesn't look up. I sit at a small coffee table on a small, uncomfortable couch. There is nothing on the table. I wait for a few minutes. Finally, the receptionist looks up and says in an exasperated way, "Can I help you?"

I say, "Yes. I'm here to see John."

"Just a minute." She calls John and says, "Someone is here to see you." She turns back to me. "Have a seat."

"Thanks," I said, and sat back down.

After ten minutes, John arrives. He shakes my hand and we walk down a grey hallway. When we pass people in the hall, they don't look up, they don't acknowledge my existence. We finally make our way to a grey, windowless conference room with Successories on the wall with sayings like "there is no I in team".

"Do you want some coffee?" John asks.

"Yes please."

"It's down the hall in the kitchen."

I walk down to the kitchen and grab a Styrofoam cup. I pour the coffee in the cup and reach for the sugar and "cream" canisters. I pour them into my cup, but the coffee is cold, so the "cream" clumps up in the cup. I try to stir it with the plastic stirrer, but finally I give up and pour it down the drain. Then, I head back to the conference room. When I arrive, John and I immediately begin the meeting.

Scenario 2: I walk into the office. When I enter, the receptionist walks from behind the desk, puts out her hand and says, "You must be Mr. Darnell. Welcome! Please have a seat and John will be with you shortly."

I sit on a comfortable couch in a beautiful, light filled lobby adorned with artwork from local artists. There is wonderful music playing. On the table in front of me are magazines and a coffee table book filled with the history of this company along with photos of projects and profiles of their people. I thumb through this beautiful book, see some beautiful buildings, and read all about their founders and leadership team.

John enters and takes me down the hall toward the conference room. Everyone we meet looks me in the eye and says hello and welcome.

We reach the conference room. It is filled with windows and more artwork. "Would you like some coffee?", John asks. "Sure", I say, "if it's not too much trouble."

Soon, two young people enter with silver trays. On one tray is a silver coffee pot, a silver creamer filled with real cream, and a silver sugar bowl filled with sugar cubes. John pours our coffee into ceramic cups that are branded with their logo and I add cream. The second tray is filled with Petit Fours, cookies, and small cakes. I take a few and place them on branded napkins. John then asks me about my travel to the office and my hotel accommodations. He offers me some tickets to their local symphony at the concert hall that they have renovated and lets me know other things I can do while I am in town. He asks me how my business is. In time, we begin our meeting.

Two questions: Which one of these scenarios is more like your company? Which company would you rather do business with?

I recently was engaged by a well-established, top 200 contractor. They were great builders, but when they hired a firm to get the pulse of owners in the area, the results were surprising to them. All owners admitted that they thought that this company built great buildings, communicated well, and were technically excellent. They also stated that this company wasn't as good with relationships, they were difficult to work with at times and were not as fun to work with as their competitors. They also added that they never heard from them between projects. They now are strategically focusing on the human side of this equation and teaching their employees these emotional intelligence principles.

A couple of the top managers from this company awaited the return of one of their executives from a meeting with a potential client. He made it all about them and did not tout schedule, price, or quality. It went very well. They have found out two very important things:

1. Every company comes to the table with schedule, price, and quality. It is not really a competitive advantage. It is the price of entry.

2. When you compete on price alone, you become a commodity, but if you create a positive experience for that client and really pay attention to your customer service, they are much more likely to choose you, even if you are not the lowest bidder.

This company is a believer. They implemented these concepts recently on a $45 million project that they were chasing. They were third on price, so they went into the presentation focusing on connecting with the selection committee. I think they thought, "Since we're not going to get this project anyway, let's do this Brent Darnell crap." They must have done a pretty good job because they were awarded the project. Since then, they have created such close connections with the company that they have been awarded an additional $35 million worth of work without bidding.

Explore how to create a positive emotional experience instead of a reliable transaction. Think about all of the ways that you can create these experiences. Tap into the intangible, emotional side of business to make your company stand out. Of course, your people will have to be trained on how to carry this initiative out. They must hone their empathy skills so that they can truly understand what is important to the project stakeholders. But once they start taking this concept and running with it, you will start to see miraculous changes internally and externally.

You will find that you are no longer competing on price alone because there are more criteria to choose from. Why do you think some owners choose on price alone? It's because they think that every contractor there will be the same pain in the ass as any other contractor. But what if they loved you? What if they couldn't imagine their lives without you? That is another criterion, and the short list for that project will likely be very small.

Chapter 8

TEAMWORK AND TRUST: HOW TO CREATE HIGH PERFORMING TEAMS ON EVERY PROJECT

Tracy Kidder, Pulitzer Prize winning author of The Soul of a New Machine, said, "Building is the quintessential act of civilization." Think about it. If three people washed up on a deserted island, the first thing they would try to do is collectively and cooperatively build a shelter. Unless the three people were an Owner's Rep, an Architect, and a Contractor. Then, they would have to wait for some lawyers to wash up on the beach to straighten everything out.

According to a June 2016 report by McKinsey & Company, large capital projects take 20% longer to finish and 80% of them are over budget. It's time to create some disruptive change and look at our projects in a whole new way.

Does anyone else find it odd that many aspects of the AEC industry, to a large extent, are based on mistrust? One survey I read said that there were only two occupations with a lower level of trust than contractors: television evangelists and used car dealers.

We work in an industry where the owner may not trust the architect or the contractor, so the work is competitively bid and perhaps a construction manager is hired just to keep an eye on things. The contractor may not trust the subcontractors, so again everything is competitively bid. When you think about it, even the term "subcontractor" seems hierarchical and demeaning and doesn't suggest a sense of cooperation. The owner and architect may not trust the contractor, so they are constantly asking for verifications of pricing and methodologies. The contractor may not trust the architect or the owner, so he documents everything that is said and done to prepare for claims and litigation. When a problem is encountered, the process, from writing requests for information (RFIs) to processing a change order, is usually filled with negotiations, conflicts, and arguments. One owner referred to RFIs as Requests for Income. The whole process is adversarial.

When I was a project manager, I was on a project where I hated the architect's representative. I don't use that word lightly. It was a horrible relationship. The drawings were flawed, and there were numerous tolerance and constructability issues. When we submitted requests for information to clarify the details, the one thing we heard over and over was, "If that's the way I drew it, that's the way I want it!" Also, we were constantly reminded that we bid the drawings the way they were.

While reviewing the drawings, I noticed that there was a symbol designated as EWC in all of the corridors of this multi-story bioscience building. I assumed it meant electric water cooler, but when I went to the legend, it said eastern water closet. I looked that up in the Kohler product guide. As it turns out, an eastern water closet is a hole in the ground with two footprints on either side so you can squat as you relieve yourself.

I called the architect's representative and asked him if he really wanted those EWCs in all of the corridors. His response was, "If that's the way I drew it, that's the way I want it!" I contacted Kohler and received a cut sheet, wrote an RFI that said, "Per your instructions, we are installing these eastern water closets in all of the corridors per the drawings." I sent it to everyone I could think of. This did not help our relationship. My biggest error was not realizing that the architect's representative was also the guy who was generating our punch list. And it was lengthy. In addition, the Architect priced the Eastern Water Closet versus the Electric Water Cooler and requested a credit since we must have bid it that way.

It becomes a game of risk. Some owners think that contractors don't assume the risk for the amount of fee. Contractors are always looking for ways to mitigate risk and much of the time the solution is to pass the risk on to trade partners. No one really knows what the real fee numbers are, so trust is rarely established.

These kinds of stories used to be numerous in the industry. Thank goodness there are less of these kinds of situations. But many of us technical folks love to be right and prove others wrong. And that mindset doesn't do much for teamwork and trust or collaboration.

Imagine if everyone in the business increased their emotional intelligence, focusing on interpersonal skills, empathy, and social responsibility. When a project was begun, true teams would be created based on mutual trust. When a request for information was written, there would be enough trust so that the problem would be identified and corrected, and the contractor would be paid a fair price for the work without all of the back and forth arguments. They would, in turn, pay all of the downstream folks their fair share.

When I was a project manager, I suggested that we start calling our subcontractors "co-contractors", but my suggestion was met with blank stares or laughter. In Europe, they call these companies "entrepreneurs". Lee Evey, the former head of the Design Build Institute of America, suggests that we call them "specialty contractors." Another term being used is trade partners. These names, as opposed to subcontractor, are much more conducive to creating a sense of team.

Think of the time and money spent on cover-your-ass documentation, disagreements, and negotiations on a project. If we could reduce this non-productive workload by creating true teams, imagine how teamwork and productivity would skyrocket. Everyone in the industry would benefit from such a shift, and everyone, including owners, architects, designers, contractors, and trade partners would be able to have more successful projects and add more to their bottom line.

A recent study by the Construction Industry Institute (ENR August 11/18, 2014) stated that "Working relationships and team dynamics have emerged as the leading variables affecting the cost and schedule of industrial projects."

One study at Penn State measured group cohesion: the degree to which the individuals on a team have shared task commitment, group pride, and interpersonal alignment. It also measured team integration: the degree to which team members from separate organizations and disciplines are engaged in collaborative activities.

The study found that 58% of over budget projects had below average levels of group cohesion. 60% of on budget projects had above average levels of group cohesion. 70% of projects delivered late had below average levels of team integration. 53% of projects delivered on time had above average levels of team integration. In short, collaboration works!

Take a look at the following graph from the Lean Construction Institute (LCI):

Organizational Aspects

Team dynamics gaps between best and typical

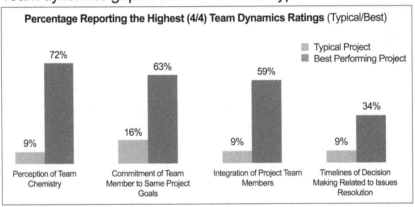

Courtesy of the Lean Construction Institute research project: *Why do Projects Excel?: The Business Case for Lean,* 2016

The LCI study showed team dynamics were much higher on best performing projects than typical projects. Perception of team chemistry was 72% on best performing and 9% on typical.

Commitment of team members to same project goals was 83% on best performing and 16% on typical. Integration of project team members was 59% on best performing and 9% on typical. Timeliness of decision making related to issue resolution was 34% on best performing and 9% on typical. This is pretty clear evidence that positive team dynamics mean project success.

Take a look at the following project where lack of teamwork and trust slowed the job progress to the point where one of the tri-venture partners knew that outside help was needed. This was a $400 million tri-venture hospital project in California. The three contractors were at each other's throats. There was a total lack of trust, gossip was running rampant, and there were several personality conflicts. Teamwork was virtually non-existent.

Analyzing the situation using a systems thinking approach, it was apparent that they had created a reinforcing loop. The lack of communication and information sharing caused team members to make assumptions, which were not always accurate. This misinformation led to a lack of trust, which caused the team members to be even more guarded with their communication and information sharing. This resulted in more mistrust, followed by even less information sharing and communication. The cycle continued to reinforce itself until they finally called us.

This reinforcing loop is known as the "downward spiral to hell". I had a dream the night before this intervention where a fistfight broke out among all of the stakeholders. It looked like one of those bar room brawls in the movies. This was not comforting, but despite my premonitions, we pressed on.

We first did an evaluation of the project team using the EQ-i® 2.0. That gave us some clues as to why they were behaving the way they were. Most had the typical construction manager's profile, which was exacerbating the conflicts. We also performed interviews with the managers from the three companies. They were using words like "always" and "never" in their descriptions of situations and people on the project. This was an indication that they were definitely caught in this downward spiral. Using this information, we created a learning program targeting relationships, communication, vision, and team building.

The first question I asked the group was, "What are the goals for this project?" There was total silence. Finally, after a minute or so, someone said, "Make money!" Okay, what else? They struggled to come up with an agreed upon list of goals. They were so caught up in the difficulties, they lost sight of what they were trying to accomplish.

Then I asked them, "If you, the leaders of this project, don't know what the goals are, what do you think about those folks in the field?" It was a real eye opener. By focusing on the people issues and how their individual emotional profile may be holding the team back, we were able to re-establish the team atmosphere and increase their productivity and effectiveness. One of the project leaders, Tracy MacDonald, a Project Director for McCarthy Construction, credited the intervention with saving the project.

There is a real push in the industry for more integrated project delivery systems with a greater focus on cooperation and teamwork as metrics for success. Integrated Project Delivery and Lean principles are tools to encourage this collaborative process. There are rules of engagement and steps to these processes. But we must make sure that we don't leave out the relationship part of that equation. We must take into account the typical emotional profile and how it relates to developing successful teams.

If you engage in an Integrated Project Delivery process or Lean process without addressing the fundamental emotional competencies of the participants, you will be setting yourself up for diminished results or failure. Remember the two pillars of lean: respect for people and continual improvement. If everyone took the EQ-i® 2.0 evaluation and created development plans that included the context of working together on a project, if they knew their deficits and how they affect their interactions with each other, then the building processes like pull planning and working out issues would be much more collaborative and therefore more successful.

This process also breaks down many barriers and brings people closer together. The lawyers will tell you that these collaborative methods are risky and that the contracts have not been worked out properly for these types of approaches. But lawyers are all about shedding risk. These collaborative project delivery methods are about sharing risk and creating great teams.

Perhaps all that project teams need is a larger context. They tend to see thousands of small tasks and very rarely get to see the big picture. Let me walk you through a true story: Picture a large renovation project on an old Home Depot. There is no signage out front, so you stop and asked several of the workers what business was going to be moving into the space. And no one knows. No one has a clue what they are working on. How much engagement can there be when they don't even know what they are building?

One fine example of this larger context took place with another leading CM firm. Instead of the usual and totally ineffective teambuilding and partnering session (standard after winning a bid for a cancer research facility) the hospital brought in a cancer researcher for the initial meeting. He told the project team and all of the stakeholders that one in three of them would develop cancer in their lifetime. This facility would be researching cures and preventive measures to reduce the number of deaths from cancer. He impressed upon them that they were building something that may someday save their life or the life of a loved one.

What a powerful, emotionally intelligent approach to the creation of a common purpose and a true sense of team! Even if you aren't building a cancer center, every structure has a purpose, whether that is creating homes for families, schools for learning, buildings for businesses to keep our economy moving, sports and entertainment venues for our pleasure, or infrastructure to help us create power, create fresh drinking water, remove our waste, or travel from place to place. You can create a personal connection on every single project that you do.

I think we have all forgotten what a complex miracle construction is. Putting a building together is one of the most complicated processes you will ever encounter. On your next project, try tapping into that higher sense of purpose and accomplishment in order to create a true sense of team.

These true teams, teams that perform at a very high level, are rare. There are many software programs that share information and supposedly promote teamwork. But do they? Could technology actually hinder teamwork? We are constantly being bombarded with information, and everyone is tethered to their phones, constantly checking for emails and voicemails. I see it when I do program work.

The Georgia Tech football team did an interesting thing in their quest for the ACC championship in 2009. They took away everyone's mobile device. Before the phone ban, the coaches found that every time that the players had a spare minute, they were on the phone, texting and communicating with others. When the phones were taken away, they started interacting with each other more and became closer as a team. What if we banned phones in offices or on projects for short periods of time and encouraged more interaction among project stakeholders? Everyone would connect more, communicate more, and create better relationships and better teams.

These high performing teams are rare, but profound when they come together. Real teams need to have mutual accountability, but with the present project delivery methods that focus on shedding risk, this is impossible. Taking this concept to a higher level, what do you suppose makes a high performing team? One of the requirements is for every team member to care about the other team members and their personal goals, growth, and development. Again, we are tapping into that emotional side of teamwork, where the members create good relationships and have the empathy skills to understand the other team members' goals and aspirations. In short, they create great relationships with each other. One of our participants put it this way, "I think relationships are very important in the construction business. Good relationships with clients mean repeat business, and good relationships with subcontractors mean successful projects."

Scott Sabin of Jacobsen Construction along with many members of his project team went through our Total Leadership Program, which teaches many of the aspects of connEx, our project-based program. Scott put it this way: "With the Total Leadership Program, all of my project teams have grown stronger and we are focused on a goal of making each other better and more effective communicators. I know that I wouldn't have been as valuable of a team member without focusing on emotional intelligence through the Total Leadership Program. I plan on using the skills I learned for many more years to come."

There is some neuroscience behind these approaches with teamwork and trust. There is a researcher named Paul Zak, a Neuroeconomist who studies oxytocin, which has been dubbed the "trust hormone" or the "connection hormone". This is the hormone released by mothers and babies when they are nursing.

Zak found that the release of this hormone is universal and creates empathy and trust. The study was designed to measure trust and trustworthiness and oxytocin levels. Participants were given $10. They could give any or all of their $10 to a stranger in the lab. And whatever they gave was tripled. This was the measurement of trust. The person receiving the money would keep it all or send all or some of it back to the sender. This was a measure of trustworthiness. 90% of the first participants sent money.

Of those who received money, 95% returned some of the money. The more money that the first participants gave, the more money that the receivers gave back. But they took the experiment further. They dosed up one group with oxytocin and one group with a placebo. The oxytocin group doubled the number of people who sent all of their money to a stranger. They also found that oxytocin increased charitable contributions by 50%.

Zak also found the "selfish hormone", which is testosterone. Testosterone blocks the action of oxytocin, creating selfishness and mistrust. Participants dosed up on testosterone not only gave less money, but they tended to use their money to punish others who they felt were being selfish.

Testosterone increases dramatically when stress levels are high, and people can become even more selfish and mistrustful. Does anyone know an industry filled with testosterone and high stress? No wonder it's difficult to create teams with high levels of trust.

Zak tells us that there are non-pharmacological ways to increase oxytocin that include massage, dancing, and praying. But the fastest way to increase oxytocin is physical touch, specifically hugs. He recommends at least eight hugs per day for better health, better relationships, and better connections with others. Now I realize we can't convince owners to have owner mandated hugs on our projects, but we can offer virtual hugs such as showing people appreciation and treating them like human beings instead of adversaries.

Beyond Partnering:

We've all been on projects with partnering agreements. You know the drill. Everyone agrees to work together, and they all sign a big partnering agreement. Then they do a group hug and start the project. After a few weeks the problems start. People start establishing territories. The personality conflicts begin. The egos become entrenched. Everyone starts finding what they missed in the contract and develops strategies to overcome the deficits, usually to the detriment of other project stakeholders. It usually devolves into a mess. Traditional partnering sessions, in our opinion, are a waste of time and money. We have developed a methodology that goes beyond, and more importantly, is more effective than the traditional partnering session and contributes to the success of all project stakeholders and the project.

It is called **connEx,** a method that connects people using emotional intelligence. That's what the "E" stands for. This method builds the people while you build the project. This process results in highly capable people and project teams that achieve outstanding results relative to safety, quality, schedule and budget. This gives you extreme performance for people and projects. We assembled the best minds in the business to create **connEx**. Lou Bainbridge, our partnering guru, Rich Seiler, our Lean guru, and Gretchen Gagel, one of the smartest strategists I know.

Here are the basics:

1) BUILD THE PEOPLE FIRST:

In order to execute the plan, we must make sure that the people are optimized as individuals and as a team. This initial focus on the people ensures that the plans are properly executed and that all team members are working together.

a) Build the people before you build the project. It is our goal to assemble as many people in the beginning as possible including owners, designers, program managers, contractors, trade partners, vendors, suppliers, facilities maintenance folks, and end users.

b) Start with an introduction to emotional intelligence and the basics of **connEx**. Everyone learns what emotional intelligence is, how it can be measured and improved, and how it relates to project and personal success. Introduce the concept of physical well-being, peak performance, and the mind-body connection and how it affects emotional, physical, and mental performance, which contribute to project success.

c) Project team members take the EQi 2.0 evaluation and Symptom Survey (physical evaluation), and a Social Style test that covers personality traits, communication preferences, and team interactions. Go over the evaluation results and how it affects team dynamics, communication, stress management, relationships, and ultimately, professional, personal and project success.

d) Each project team member will create their own professional, personal, health, and project goals. This is an ideal time to focus on areas in the project stakeholders' personal lives that they want to change - finances, health, a new hobby, quitting smoking, eating better, etc. Everyone will have accountability partners to help hold them accountable to create these changes. Individual and project coaches are vital for the success of these projects and can be internal.

e) Determine the group scores and address any group developmental needs as well as the project needs.

f) NOTE: It is highly recommended that this process be a week-long to two-week-long retreat that connects the team in an irrevocable and profound way. Beyond team building, there is a focus on intense planning and value stream mapping where everyone agrees on project metrics. Then, all stakeholders are taught the basics of stress management, time management, exercise, sleep, and nutrition. This may seem ridiculous to some of you hard-nosed construction folks. There is a reason for this recommendation.

From my experience implementing and managing leadership programs for an ENR top 5 CM firm, I consistently saw that teams really came together during the middle of the second week. If you can't do two weeks, do a week. If you can't do a week, do a weekend. If you can't do a weekend, do a day. If you can't do a day, then during the first month of the project, do half days of the people stuff every single day. The other recommendation for these extended retreats is no cell phones or computers and no checking in at work. There is something miraculous that happens after three days without electronics. Ideas start flowing. Mental, physical, and emotional health returns, creativity flourishes and people connect with each other to form an amazing team.

2) PLAN FOR SUCCESS:

Establish an overall plan with the input of as many stakeholders as possible with milestones and metrics.

a) Establish meeting ground rules, project mission statement, shared values, critical success factors, team metrics, and rocks in the road. This includes the entire life cycle of the project from concept to demolition or re-use. This includes design, construction, commissioning/turnover, and facilities maintenance.

b) Use the Last Planner System™ to create a meaningful project plan that drives value, eliminates waste, and improves the entire process. Prior to the Last Planner process, begin Step 1, Build the People. Create the trust and relationships first so that the Last Planner System™ process goes smoothly with open, honest information sharing. There is a focus on collaboration from the very beginning, and there is an integrated form of agreement signed by all parties. For Owners who cannot sign an integrated form of agreement, find the most collaborative contract that is appropriate to that Owner.

3) MEASURE FOR SUCCESS AND ADJUST:

Every person has individual goals and the project has project goals that are agreed to by all parties. These metrics are meticulously tracked and adjustments are made to ensure success.

a) All team members agree on project goals and key performance indicators such as schedule, budget, quality, safety, turnover, training, facilities maintenance, and end user requirements. Identify hot buttons for all project stakeholders, the things that keep them up at night, and track them as well. Take the group through project goals so that everyone is clear on the overall goals and how their personal goals and company goals tie into this entire process. Discuss the basics of communication, roles, and responsibilities for each project stakeholder and company.

b) Once these metrics are established, vigorously track them with a cloud-based tracking tool. We recommend The Client Feedback Tool or the Organizational Health Index.

c) There is a constant evaluation of project metrics and project needs. Do they have the right resources? During the Lean weekly work plan and update, determine what is holding up work. Check your constraint log. If there is a problem, it's likely one of the following:

> Tools
> Information
> Materials
> Manpower
> Equipment
> Safety
> Space

TIMMES courtesy of Unified Works *www.unified-works.com*

d) You can also use a customized list similar to the Gallup 12 questions so that every person knows all of the resources needed to move the work forward. This information ties into the Last Planner System™ and the near-term schedules. This constant feedback loop assures minimum down time and schedule delays due to a lack of resources. Continuously track and adjust.

e) Also follow up with every individual and their plans. Are they making progress? Do they need more accountability and coaching?

f) Resource allocation and flow are critical to the success of the project, and this will be a top priority for the project team, to ensure that all resources are available when they are needed.

g) Project Team Health Assessment: Set metrics for the key performance indicators for personal and project success and measure these metrics throughout the project with your tracking tool.

h) When you check the metrics (at least monthly), make adjustments on what is not working and celebrate what is working. Every individual will also track progress on their personal goals and meet with their accountability partner often. Have coaches available to meet individuals for coaching sessions as required.

i) There is much accountability built into this process. Set up cross-function accountability partners. For instance, the architect representative might be the accountability partner of a contractor's project manager. The owner's representative might be the accountability partner of a superintendent. They hold each other accountable throughout the course of the project for reaching both personal and project goals.

4) HIGH PERFORMING PEOPLE CREATE HIGH PERFORMING TEAMS:

When every individual is performing at their highest level mentally, physically and emotionally, and these individuals are aligned in the execution of a perfect project outcome, the project can't help but be successful.

a) This preliminary work with emotional intelligence and peak physical performance give participants a better understanding of themselves, their limitations, and where to improve. There are some great initial exercises to set a baseline. One is called the Four Quadrants which is included in Appendix A: Resources. You can also download the 4 Quadrants by visiting *www.brentdarnell. com/resources*. Participants divide a piece of flip chart paper into four quadrants and label them family, this project,

119

personal, and future vision. At the top, they put their name and their favorite piece of music. At the bottom, they put some of their challenges for the project, personally, and professionally. This is a great exercise. It breaks down barriers and creates a lot of emotional threads among the participants. Track this information for each individual forever so you can check in occasionally to see what has changed. You can also revisit this exercise at the end of the project.

b) Have all project stakeholders write a letter to themselves dated the last day of the project that lists all of their accomplishments that they have attained as a result of the program as well as the results of the project. This future diary plants all of their accomplishments and project success in their subconscious so that even if they aren't thinking about them consciously, they are still working on them. You can also give the participants the option of making a mind movie, which is a visual future diary. One other idea is to make a mind movie for the project showing tangible outcomes. What if people could see this perfect project with no punch list and happy clients and stakeholders at the beginning and throughout the project. With the magic of movies, you can create something spectacular and watch it when times get tough.

c) Individuals can track peak performance progress by taking the Body Battery Inventory (Appendix A: Resources) or by downloading it at:

www.brentdarnell.com/resources

This evaluation tracks stressors and recovery activities to ensure that the individual is keeping an eye on all of the things that contribute to peak mental, physical, and emotional performance.

d) Teach everyone how to coach each other. There is a simple methodology called Outcome Coaching. Project stakeholders perform peer-to-peer coaching and group coaching, using the project as a backdrop and catalyst to help each other attain all of their goals and overcome any issues. It is in Appendix A: Resources and at this link: *www.brentdarnell.com/resources*

5) ENSURE PROJECT SUCCESS:

Supports the project and all stakeholders throughout the duration of the project. Offer continuous monitoring, 24/7 coaching (internally and/or externally), and ongoing learning that supports the project goals and individual goals. This ensures the greatest possible chance of success for every single project.

a) Deliver learning modules spread throughout the project on various topics such as team-building, innovation, communication, relationships, stress management, peak performance, time management, presentation skills, innovation, and problem solving. All of these sessions should be in the context of the project, so you can address anything that is getting off track.

Utilize reflective learning continually because repetition creates retention. Reflect each week you meet upon personal success and project success and measure the metrics that we have designated to determine progress. This ongoing learning and checking in ensures success of individuals and the project.

b) This process ensures project success by maximizing the potential of every single person on the project, creating measurable metrics for individuals and the project that are continuously tracked, and making adjustments throughout the project to maximize project success.

High performing teams are a thing of beauty when they come together. So how do you create high performing teams on every project? The answer is twofold: 1. Be deliberate with your approach and 2. Focus on the people. You may not be able to do everything in connEx, but if you implement as much as you can, you will see results. The more elements, the better chance you have of creating a high performing team.

You may be asking yourself, "What is the return on investment?" Although this is difficult to ascertain, we can see from several industry studies from CII, LCI and Penn State that collaboration works and saves both time and money. You will have to decide what that magic number is to spend on these types of programs, but the important thing is to begin. Whether you are a large, medium, or small company, start where you can and build upon your successes. Modify these concepts based on budget and culture and project and see where it takes you.

Chapter 9

QUALITY, PRODUCTIVITY, INNOVATION, AND LEAN

How many times does work-in-place have to be removed because of other work that has been installed out of sequence? How many times does the communication break down and cause something to be delivered late or installed incorrectly? How many times do we improperly handle the architect's and the owner's expectations only to be ambushed during closeout and forced into reworking the finishes?

The Construction Industry Institute's research estimates that re-work costs on average 5% of total construction costs. This is money that is being robbed from your bottom line. During the Total Quality Management revolution and the six-sigma sojourns of the 80s and 90s, manufacturers vastly increased their productivity and decreased their defect rates. Unfortunately, the AEC industry was virtually bypassed by that whole revolution. Productivity on most projects, even well managed projects, has been far lower than most manufacturers. In a recent productivity survey by FMI, a leading construction industry consultant, "53% of the respondents said that productivity had remained the same, decreased slightly or decreased substantially over the past five years."

Low quality is also an issue on most projects because productivity and quality go hand in hand. One could argue that it is easier to control these factors in a manufacturing setting where there are repetitive work processes. This is undeniably true. One can also argue that by exploring new, innovative methods, productivity and quality on construction projects can be dramatically increased.

There are many tools and methods out there that are supposed to improve quality and productivity: Integrated Project Delivery, Lean, Design Build, building information modeling (BIM), web-based information sharing tools, computer-aided design systems, augmented and virtual reality, drones, personal and handheld computers, tablets, smartphones, apps, digital cameras, lasers, automated transits, and project management and accounting software. And though they do improve productivity to some extent, how do we make that quantum leap to achieve the same high quality and productivity numbers as manufacturers? We must take a fresh look at everything about our business. We keep trying to maximize results of processes that are decades old instead of coming up with new processes and products that will provide breakthroughs.

Lean is making a lot of headway in the industry. Lean is a manufacturing process that creates flow and eliminates waste with continual improvement. We have taken these concepts and applied them to construction. The two pillars of lean are respect for people and continual improvement. In this industry we focus heavily on the process and tend to forget about the people side. But without the people side, the process falls apart. We have created a lean boot camp that addresses both. If your lean programs don't address both, maybe it's time to go back and take another look.

And what about innovation? Innovation is a huge key for remaining competitive, yet most companies don't consciously promote innovation. How much does the industry invest in research and development? How many companies make a conscious effort to promote innovation? Why do you think that is? Take a look at the typical emotional profile for construction managers. Many have the control profile (low flexibility, high problem solving, and high reality testing) which causes them to be rigid in their approaches. This may serve them well in many ways such as adhering to plans and specifications, but with this rigid way of thinking, there is little innovation. New ideas are met with skepticism and rejection. We are all too gun-shy with risk. We can't try anything new. What if it doesn't work? A new product? An innovative approach to building? Let the other guy take the risk. This is also true for individuals. You learn quickly not to come to your boss with a new idea.

How many times do you hear the following?:
We've always done it that way.
We tried that, but it didn't work.
Why try something new?
Let's not take the risk.
Just do it the way I told you to do it.

Most employees in the AEC industry are linear thinkers who are not great innovators. So how do you cultivate a creative environment? By promoting innovation and creative thinking. We are all creative thinkers to varying degrees, but most technical folks would label themselves as not creative. This simply isn't true. Creativity is like a muscle. The more you work it, the better you are able to create. Companies should offer classes in creative thinking and innovation.

There is an exercise called "Yes, and ...". It is an applied improvisation exercise. We go around the table and each person states his idea about any subject, say improving innovation at the company? And the person next to them will say, "Yes, but ..." and fill in the blank: it's too expensive, no one will ever do that, that's stupid, we tried that in 2005 and it didn't work. As technical people, we are trained to find problems. We are used to saying, "Yes, but... " People at the table find out pretty quickly that Yes butting ideas is pretty demoralizing. Think about it this way: what if a loved one asked you if you loved them and you replied, "Yes, but..."

Then we do the exercise again only this time, the response is "Yes, and... " You must acknowledge the other person's idea. It doesn't mean you agree with them or even that it is a good idea. It simply means that you honor that person and build on their idea. The change in the energy of the room is palpable. The ideas flow freely. Keep in mind that some of the ideas will be pretty outrageous, but these are what lead to really innovative ideas that can be implemented.

During one of these exercises for a small company, they "yes, anded" a trip to Las Vegas for the entire company. The President looked at me with a scowl on his face. He said this was a ridiculous exercise and there was no way in hell he was going to pay for a trip to Las Vegas. Then, his Executive Assistant said, "I know we can't all go to Las Vegas, but we could have a casino night at the office and raise money for a charity." They would have never reached that idea if they had not "yes anded" and explored some outrageous possibilities. When you do a "yes, and" exercise, explore the most outrageous idea and ask yourself what is the idea behind the idea. For instance, a group "yes anded" kegs of beer at every desk. The idea behind the idea was to loosen up and have more fun at work. Then, explore the reasonable ways you can do that.

From an emotional standpoint, individuals with high problem-solving skills and reality testing along with low flexibility, tend to be very rigid in their approaches to things. By working on flexibility and offering different ways of thinking about problem solving, we can improve the creativity and innovation of even the most rigid, linear thinkers.

Companies can also create environments that are more conducive to creativity. They can routinely do brainstorming sessions and panel discussions to explore new ways of doing business and innovative ways to approach projects. These groups should have a mix of young and old, newcomers and veterans. In these sessions, nothing should be censored, nothing should be too far-fetched. Once everyone starts participating in these processes, you will notice an increase in creative ideas, which will add to your competitive edge.

If you take a look at the typical EI profile, you can see that if you improve the project stakeholders' emotional intelligence, especially in the areas of empathy, relationships, flexibility, and problem-solving skills, we can improve quality, productivity, and innovation dramatically. Think about it. Many productivity problems on construction projects are caused by poor communication and poor relationships.

Many quality control issues are due to poor communication and preparation and have little to do with expertise. High quality has more to do with motivating the workers to perform the work properly and managing the expectations of the owner and architect. Innovation is about creating environments where people feel safe to explore the possibilities. This is directly tied to the social competence of your project team.

Consider this apartment project where the mechanical, electrical, plumbing, and fire protection trade partners had very poor working relationships. The project had a densely packed hallway (is there any other kind?), in which the sprinkler contractor had to install his work prior to the ductwork, or his access would be cut off. The sprinkler contractor was behind and had not installed his piping. The duct man installed his ductwork anyway, knowing that the sprinkler man would have to pay him to take the duct down and reinstall it.

When the superintendent asked the duct man why he did it, he replied, "I got mine in per the schedule." The superintendent pressed him further. "Didn't you notice that the sprinkler man hadn't installed his work?" His reply was, "F#@! him! I've got a schedule to keep. If I had been late, you would have jumped all over my ass."

You can see several problems with this exchange. There was general lack of trust and communication among all of the stakeholders on the project, from the general contractor to the subcontractors. It caused much re-work, decreased quality and productivity, and ate into everyone's project fee.

Emotional intelligence can be used to improve productivity and the quality of the final product. It occurred on a housing project for the 1996 Olympic village in Atlanta, Georgia, which was being built for the state of Georgia (Georgia State Financing and Investment Commission or GSFIC). At that time, the GSFIC's contracts were difficult and their closeout procedures extremely demanding. Many of their projects took over a year after the certificate of occupancy to close out and receive final payment.

The project team had taken the time to do a lot of teambuilding and cultivated great relationships among the mechanical, electrical, plumbing, and fire protection trade partners. We created shirts that put the name of all trade partners on it along with the caption GOING FOR THE GOLD! This project had a similar situation, a packed hallway in which the sprinkler man needed to install his work prior to the duct. The schedule was accelerated due to some weather-related delays, but the sprinkler contractor was not aware of this change.

The duct man had a great relationship with the foreman for the sprinkler company, and they often went out after work for a beer. Instead of installing his ductwork ahead of the sprinkler contractor, the duct man notified the sprinkler guy, and they worked out a way to install their work per the schedule, saving re-work and time. This great teamwork contributed to a highly successful project for all of these stakeholders.

In the end, the project was completed ahead of schedule despite seventeen straight days of rain during the foundation work and a damaging fire half way through the project. The key to the success of this project was relationships. Great relationships contributed to great productivity despite many setbacks.

Expectations of the GSFIC and the architect were managed so that everyone knew what to expect at the end of the project with regard to levels of quality. This resulted in a quick closeout. In fact, the project was closed out within thirty days, which was extremely rare for GSFIC projects. The average closeout for GSFIC projects for our company at the time was eighteen months.

Probably one of the biggest time wasters in the industry is meetings. Why do we have meetings? Think about the topics that are covered at most meetings. Do you focus on positive, productive issues such as teambuilding, vision, relationships, celebrations of milestones, celebrations of project goals, and other human aspects of the project? Or do you focus more on the crises and problems such as conflicts between contractors, owner and architect problems, non-performance issues, poor communication, relationship issues, and cover-your-ass posturing?

If the majority of your meetings are taken up with the latter, you may want to take a different approach. If you work to improve the people side of your project that promotes great relationships and positive communication, you will spend less time on the problems. Try taking a different approach to meetings. Always have a timed agenda, a time-keeper and facilitator, and make sure you add some items that build team morale and take more of a long-term view. This will make your meetings more productive and enjoyable. In addition, if you start with something fun, the meetings are more likely to be full of energy and engagement.

You may want to also try Lean Coffee meetings, where the meeting format is streamlined, and everyone gets to contribute. It's a very simple meeting process based on the Lean model.

Stress and burnout can negatively affect productivity. When we are tired and stressed, we aren't nearly as productive. When we work past our effective limits, productivity decreases. Some studies effectively argue that you can do more by working less. For many people in the AEC industry, this is a hard concept to embrace. But according to one study, working past the point of fatigue increases problem-solving time by as much as 500%. How many times have you pushed yourself to complete a task only to have to do it all over again the next day? When you are tired, it is much better to take short, focused breaks in order to restore yourself and be more productive.

Bryan Smith, a Superintendent with The Beck Group tells this story about productivity for masons on a project. The masons lived far away from the project and their time at home was being compromised. Bryan states, "The production rate was not what the Superintendent was looking for while working a bunch of overtime to "catch up". Actually, the production rate declined disproportionately to the extra hours. They were working six ten-hour days and the brick average was lower than what should have been the yield, given the number of hours. We decided to change the work hours to four, ten-hour days and two, eight hour days for two weeks, then five, eight hour days for the third week. This equals a 16% decrease in hours over the three-week span, but also yielded a 15% increase in bricks laid over the same time period."

There was an article in the *Harvard Business Review (June 2010)* concerning Sony's efforts to make their employees more productive. What they found was that by taking more breaks and building in more recovery times throughout the day, their employees were much more engaged and productive. This was a hard sell to management, but the results are undeniable. Employees now take their lunches and build in uninterrupted time for important tasks and setting the course. They focus on four areas: physical health through nutrition, sleep, daytime renewal, and exercise; emotional well-being and feeling valued and appreciated; mental clarity including the ability to focus and think creatively; and spiritual significance so that employees feel that what they are doing is important and goes beyond just profit.

I worked with one company who had a policy that their employees must keep their phones on twenty-four hours a day, seven days a week. I sat in a meeting with one of these employees who answered his phone five times during a one-hour meeting. This may seem like a good thing for customer service, but what is the cost to the employees? What kind of image does this project to other stakeholders? Ask yourself what percentage of phone calls are directly related to your customers' needs? Then ask yourself what percentage of phone calls are low priority time wasters and stress makers? Do you really need to be on call every waking moment?

Smart companies are starting to pay attention to this lack of down time and stress-related issues and are offering a variety of solutions. Morning exercises stimulate the body and mind. Building in scheduled break times help employees to be more alert and focused when they return to work. Employees are encouraged to turn off their phones at these times so they are not constantly bombarded with work. Instead of working through lunches and scheduled breaks, employees are encouraged to have true downtime in order to recover and be more productive.

These group breaks also help with relationships and teambuilding, creating high-performing teams that naturally have higher productivity. By working well together they manage these relationship issues and minimize conflicts that interfere with productivity. They spend less time on non–productive activities and more time on activities that create meaningful results.

Quality and productivity improve when we focus on people, and if productivity rises even by a few percentage points, margins increase dramatically. Take a look at the following example: You have a $25,000,000 project with $10,000,000 in labor costs and $1,000,000 profit. If you improve your productivity by 10%, your labor costs drop to $9,000,000. This would give you a profit of $2,000,000. In other words, with a 10% increase in productivity, you could double your profit!

We talked in a previous chapter about taking a fresh approach to how we design and build buildings. In China, they put up a fifty-seven-story building in 19 days through modularization, prefabrication, and a lot of pre-planning and innovation. This building started with a cleared site and was move-in ready in 19 days. And it isn't a cheap, crappy building. It is well made, energy efficient, sustainable, and earthquake resistant. Now I understand that China has unlimited resources and that the video I watched on You Tube is likely a lot of propaganda. And there is no mention of costs per square foot.

But even with all of the doubts about putting up a fifty-seven-story building in 19 days, we must go back to the drawing board, look at a blank slate, and reinvent the way we design and build projects. It must be a joint effort. Everyone must participate. Everyone that has anything to do with the process from developers to owners to designers to contractors to trade partners to facilities managers to construction product companies to labor unions to government entities to power generators must be involved. All of the industry groups must weigh in: AGC, ABC, CURT, CII, COAA, CMAA, ASCE, USGBC, and many others.

We must all contribute our knowledge to come up with better ways to build projects. We must bring every innovation and technological advancement to bear including 3D printing, the internet of things, artificial intelligence, laser scanning, drones, robotics, prefabrication, modularization, and collaborative project delivery. Talk about innovation! It is a Mount Everest of endeavors, but we can do it. There are a lot of smart people out there. And when we put our heads together, we can improve everything about our business. It's time for a major change!

Chapter 10

COMMUNICATION AND KNOWLEDGE SHARING

Knowledge is a firm's most valuable resource. According to the National Academy of Sciences Task Force on Intellectual Property Management, more than 75% of the capitalization of the top companies in the United States is through knowledge and other intangible assets. This is especially true in the AEC industry where employee knowledge has great economic value. In fact, in most cases, it is our only competitive edge.

Lack of communication and knowledge management are closely related to poor productivity partly because they stifle innovation and problem solving. Until we tap into the emotional side of these issues, we will be unable to increase knowledge sharing and create true learning organizations. There is a great warm-up exercise called the Big Egg Drop. Everyone divides into groups and sees who can build the least expensive contraption that will catch a raw egg. After this exercise, everyone is asked the question: "If we built this egg catcher again right now, could you build it cheaper, faster, better?"

Invariably they say "yes". But isn't this also true of our industry? Although each structure is different, the building components are fairly consistent. Do the knowledge and the lessons learned make their way to each new project? The usual answer is "not very often". The Construction Industry Institute and other organizations and companies have created a great knowledge base filled with best practices and lessons learned. These organizations find out shortly that their use is limited. Why is this? It is because people will only share information with someone they know and trust.

A large energy company learned this difficult lesson. They spent millions of dollars on knowledge sharing technology, but their employees were still not sharing their knowledge. They finally realized that technology was not the answer. Instead, they cultivated great relationships among their employees, which provided a web of knowledge that was available anytime. As their CEO put it, "Since sharing knowledge is important only at the point and time when people need to solve a problem, the key to knowledge management is connecting people in a dialogue."

Carol Hagen of Hagen Business Systems and a Bluebeam expert (hagenbusiness.com) combines technology with knowledge transfer. When she is training groups, she pairs older and younger learners who teach each other. The older learner wants to learn about the technology. The younger learner wants the older person's practical knowledge and wisdom. Everyone wins!

Sometimes technology may actually hinder productivity. It enables you to hate people faster with more anonymity. I was talking to the president of a very successful project management software company about this issue. Although they have a great web-based software product that provides links for sharing information, some contractors still blame them for the lack of communication on a project. This software company is starting to realize that sharing information is not about the technology. It's about the relationships among the project stakeholders. Some companies have even created the position of knowledge broker to connect people within the company in order to share knowledge more effectively.

The basics of communication such as speaking clearly, enunciating, listening, being fully present, being aware of your body language, facial expressions, vocal qualities are not our best things because of the typical EI profile (higher assertiveness and independence, lower emotional expression and empathy). There is an exercise called using compassion to connect. It's a simple, empathy exercise. I ask participants to think of someone they are in conflict with. It's very easy to come up with this example. Then, with that person in mind, they say the following statements:

- "Just like me, this person is trying to find happiness and meaning in his/her life."

- "Just like me, this person is trying to avoid pain in his/her life."

- "Just like me, this person has known heartache, loss, loneliness and despair."

- "Just like me, this person wants to be loved and connected with others."

- "Just like me, this person has people in his/her life who care about them."

- "Just like me, this person is trying to get his/her needs met."

- "Just like me, this person is trying his/her best to complete this project, make a profit, etc."

- "Just like me, this person is trying his/her best to make this project successful."

- "Just like me, this person wants to excel and be good at what he/she does."

- "Just like me, this person is learning about how to navigate through this sometimes-difficult life/project/work environment."

We also focus on challenging mental models, avoiding gossip, and avoiding "why" questions. When you ask someone a "why" question, most of the time, they get defensive. What you find is that you can ask that question a number of ways without "why". An example: If you asked someone, "Why did you change that detail?" The person will automatically get defensive and try to defend the change. But what if you said, "Tell me about this detail and the changes that you made." It's a completely different response. I think we should change the five "whys" for root cause analysis to the five "tell me about this in more detail" statements.

If we create these personal connections, if we establish true emotional threads, the employees will be more likely to seek advice and counsel from each other and create true learning organizations. If we cultivate the sharing of knowledge and innovative thinking, employees will contribute much more. This will ultimately contribute to increased innovation and productivity, higher margins, better projects, and a more robust bottom line.

Chapter 11

DIVERSITY AND INCLUSION AND MULTI-CULTURAL ISSUES

I speak at many industry conferences, and the rooms are usually filled with mostly middle-aged, white men. Not that I don't love middle-aged white men. I am a middle-aged white man. Fortunately for our industry, we are seeing changes in the cultural and gender makeup of our work force. Many companies are expanding their geographic areas not only in the United States, but internationally. There are more cultures represented. More women are entering the workforce. In short, we are encountering more and more diversity in this melting pot of construction.

Let's define diversity and inclusion. It is not a plea to hire more women and minorities. That is a symptom of a far larger problem of inclusion and embracing differences and new ways of doing things. Diversity is easy to define. The more diverse your teams are in terms of gender, ethnicity, education background, age, and many other factors, the better the team performs. Inclusion is about making <u>everyone</u> feel welcomed and giving them an opportunity to contribute their best ideas and do what is good.

How does this affect the way we work? Are we prepared for these diverse cultures with their different values? Are we prepared to have more women in managerial roles? Are we ready to include all of those groups who look, act, and think differently? As companies are finding out, it's not just about learning another language or reading the book, *Men Are from Mars, Women Are from Venus*. It's not just about participating in movements like 'Me, Too" and "Black Lives Matter". Many different aspects of diversity and inclusion affect the way we interact and do business.

The United States is made up of many cultures, and they all have different values and unique ways of working. Their sense of time and punctuality, their work ethic, and their priorities concerning family, work, and personal time can vary a great deal. They will likely respond differently to situations in the workplace. If companies want to be more effective, they must recognize these cultural differences and try to make adjustments to accommodate them. It may be impossible to accommodate all situations in any given group, but we must make the effort to be aware of these differences and do the best we can.

There are also regional cultures in the United States. Doing business in the north is very different than doing business in the south. In the north, people tend to be more direct and assertive. In the south, this is seen as negative behavior. Southerners refer to these Northerners as "Yankees". It is not an affectionate term. Companies in Florida and the west coast tend to have a much more casual workplace than companies in the northeast.

These cultural differences must be taken into account when doing business. These regional differences can be disastrous. One of my old bosses was a "Yankee" from the north and tended to be aggressive and blunt. We were presenting to a school board to build a school in South Georgia. We all drove down from Atlanta with our suits and ties and our well-rehearsed, slick, PowerPoint presentation.

When we arrived, the school board greeted us. Their dress was extremely casual. In fact, one of the board members, a farmer in the area, was dressed in overalls. Our "Yankee" lead presenter was blunt and abrasive and talked much too quickly. We came across like a bunch of "city-slickers" with our fancy computer presentation, trying to take advantage of these poor country folk. We would have been better off leaving the "Yankee" at home, dressing casually, establishing rapport with the board, and doing our presentation with posters.

For those companies working internationally, this cultural awareness is even more vital. Working in Europe, Russia, Latin America, and Southeast Asia involves a different set of rules. There are issues with bribery and corruption and other values. In China, "yes" doesn't necessarily mean "yes". It may only mean "I understand what you are saying". In addition, "saving face" is of prime importance. In Russia, you must be prepared to pay a "consultant" who will guide you through the intricacies of working there.

In the United States, we tend to be obsessed with time and punctuality. We like to dive right into meetings and try to reach a result in a short period of time. In Latin America, there is a more relaxed view of time. They also value intimate business relationships, which are cultivated over time. You would never discuss business during the first meeting there. These thoughtful cultural approaches are crucial for successful projects and penetrating new markets.

I facilitated a program with a group of thirty construction managers from Argentina. We had a tight schedule, and I insisted that everyone come back from breaks "on time". The problem was that fifteen minutes past the time to resume, not one person had returned. I was trying to impose my US notion of "on time" on them. I finally got the message and adjusted the schedule based on their culture, because no matter what the consequence, they never came into the room at the scheduled time. I found out that in their culture, "on time" means up to thirty minutes past the agreed upon time.

We also created a different daily schedule. In their culture, they tend to start later and finish later. The 6:00 am yoga simply did not work for this group. We started around 9:00 am and did not eat dinner until around 9:00 pm. Making these adjustments when possible allows you to obtain the highest productivity from these different cultures. We must learn to ask ourselves, "Is it wrong or just different?"

The most multi-cultural program I've ever done was with a company called Nobia, a kitchen manufacturer, supplier, installer based in Sweden. This was a group of twenty-nine people from nine different countries. I was the only American. The first thing we talked about was cultural differences. Not only did we discuss country culture, but company culture as well.

Using a North American normative group, these cultural differences show up in the EQ-i® 2.0. The Argentines (30 male Civil Engineers) scored very high in assertiveness, but low in independence. It's a macho society, but also one with a high-power distance. The boss tends to be dictatorial and autocratic. The Chinese tend to score low in independence and assertiveness. The Europeans tend to score low in social responsibility because the governments take care of the disenfranchised. The Germans scored low in flexibility.

Once we had this discussion, we soon realized that there were some generalizations that were based on real experiences, and some generalizations that were not exactly true. We also realized that we were all human beings and had much more in common than we realized. All had some form of family. All had similar struggles. We capitalized on all of the things we had in common and shattered the generalizations and minimized the differences that kept us apart.

One of the exercises for multi-cultural groups is called "the book title". I have a book for boys called *How to Be the Best at Everything*. I thought this summed up our American Culture very well. There is a touch of arrogance in that title and a real can-do attitude, which is so American. So, we divided into country groups and they had to come up with a book title that indicated their culture. The Swedes came up with *How to Be a Good Citizen and Not Stand Out*. The Germans came up with *How to Be Effective and Efficient*. The French and Spanish both came up with *How to Enjoy Life*. It's fun to see the different nation's take on society and culture.

Also, it was very interesting to see the participants as they used this discussion as a way to develop their emotional competencies such as empathy and self-awareness. This work brings diverse groups of people very close together in a relatively short period.

Some say business is business the world over, but smart companies are paying attention to the cultural dimensions of the places where they are working by making the necessary adjustments. Lack of understanding of other cultures can turn business triumphs into disasters.

Consider the story of the American entrepreneur who was getting ready to close the deal and sign the contract for a manufacturing facility in Russia. This American was a Mormon and didn't drink alcohol. In Russia, deals are customarily sealed with a vodka toast. The American served soft drinks. Because he did not embrace this honored custom of their culture, the Russians cancelled the deal.

Another cultural disaster took place when a Swedish construction company acquired a company in Poland. Poland, being a former Soviet country, had a very different culture. The bosses were stern and dictatorial. The boss told the workers what to do, and the workers did so without question. The Swedes, on the other hand, were very consensus-driven. They relied on the group to come up with the correct answers. This company sent some Swedish managers to Poland. Not knowing the culture, the Swedish managers had meetings with the Polish workers and asked for their input and ideas. The Polish workers assumed that the Swedes were inept. From their point of view, these foreign managers were so stupid; they were asking the workers to provide the answers! The Swedish managers lost the respect of the workers, and this initial setback took quite some time to overcome.

Where does this lack of understanding originate? Is it a matter of studying cultures, reading history and learning the language? Those efforts will certainly help, but these misunderstandings go beyond that. With the typical contractor's EI profile, employees may have an even more difficult time because of their low empathy and low interpersonal relationships skills. To be able to navigate these differences, employees must develop these areas.

Jonas, a project manager from Sweden, put it this way, "When moving to a new job in a new country I needed to make people feel comfortable to tell me the truth. There were a lot of problems, which needed to be identified and solved. By using emotional intelligence, I think I got a good response, and I could, therefore, take quick action in creating a new structure."

Take a look at the demographics in the industry. There are certainly many minorities working in the field, but at management levels, it's mostly white males. It is not very diverse. According to the National Association of Women in Construction, there are very few women in this male dominated industry, and the women who are in the industry are mostly in sales and office positions (56%). Those in management positions (23%) have to walk a fine line between assertiveness and compliance. If a woman is too assertive, she may be labeled a "bitch". If she is too compliant, she may get little respect.

We must learn to utilize the strengths of these talented women and embrace different approaches to project management. We must not only accept these women in these roles, we must pursue these women, hire them, train them, and give them opportunities with a deliberate diligence. That will make our companies even more effective. In an article in Engineering News Record (November 15, 2010), they showed empirical data on women's role in business success. They cited studies by Catalyst LLC, a research firm. They found that "companies with more women board members significantly outperformed those with fewer female directors in return on equity, return on sales, and return on invested capital." Women will make up 50% of the overall future workforce, and all industries will be competing for them. It would be wise to think about how companies can entice women to enter the AEC industry.

Smart companies are combating this diversity issue with diversity training. We must take a hard look at conscious and unconscious biases and how to overcome them. We must also focus on specific things companies can do to promote more diversity and inclusion. But the industry's lack of diversity and inclusion is a symptom of a far larger issue that ties into the typical emotional intelligence profile for construction folks.

Let's take a look again at the male/female EQ-i® 2.0:

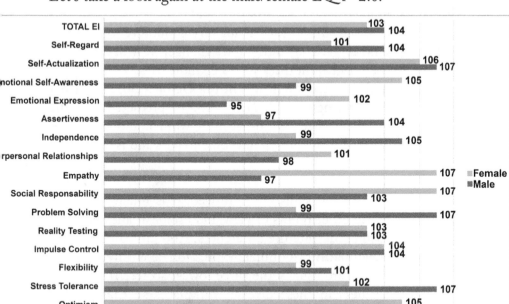

Men tend to have lower emotional self-awareness, lower empathy, which prevents us from truly connecting with others. We also see the control/perfectionist profile (lower flexibility, higher reality testing and problem solving). The result is that we aren't adept at change and new ways of working. Opening up our industry to more women and minorities is a big change that we will continue to struggle with until we work on our emotional competence. At the same time, women are more adept emotionally at collaboration and teamwork. Note the high interpersonal relationships, empathy and social responsibility. We need these women to thrive in this new industry.

I did a recent survey for minorities and women asking them the question, "As a woman/minority/LGBT, what is your biggest challenge. Some of the responses were heartbreaking, almost dehumanizing. We have to be more aware of how we act and how people perceive us as an industry. We must be more inclusive and open to new ideas and new folks entering our workforce.

If companies don't address these underlying emotional issues diversity training can be a waste of time and money. These attitudes toward women and minorities are not very conducive to a diverse workforce. And if these attitudes don't change, we will lose these capable women and minorities to other industries. We could be driving away the future. An article in the October 30, 2000 (that was a while ago) Engineering News Record predicted that the AEC industry would need to attract more women and minorities in order to grow. This prediction has come to pass and is even more true today.

Once these emotional skills are improved, it is much easier for employees to see other points of view and establish and maintain good relationships, despite the differences. And unfortunately, for most groups, empathy, emotional expression and interpersonal relationship skills are usually the three lowest scores. This is vital for doing business in these diverse workplaces so that we can create more of a team atmosphere and make our workforces more productive. This higher productivity will lead to a less stressful working environment, more successful projects, and a better bottom line.

Chapter 12

SUSTAINABILITY AND ENVIRONMENTAL ISSUES

According to the United States Green Building Council, the demand for "green" buildings continues to rise in the United States and around the world. This increase is fueled by the advantages that green buildings have over conventional construction. The buildings are more energy efficient, conserve water and resources, have lower long-term maintenance costs, and generally last longer than conventional buildings.

There are advantages to the occupants as well. Studies show that they are more productive and have fewer sick days. They experience better indoor air quality, more natural lighting, and more comfortable work environments.

An ENR article dated July 3, 2018, a study on indoor air quality at Saint Gobain's headquarters revealed boost in productivity, health and well-being, increased concentration and a decrease in back pain.

According to Annie R. Pearce, PhD., Program Director, Sustainable Facilities and Infrastructure Program at Georgia Tech, in a California study, a school was converted to a day-lit school with the addition of skylights. After the conversion, the students performed 5% to 14% better on reading, language, and math skills as measured by the California Achievement Test. In a hospital study by the University of Pittsburgh, surgery patients in rooms with natural lighting needed less pain medication.

This green building trend also has advantages to contractors. By reducing, re-using, and recycling materials, contractors can save a bundle of money on their waste removal costs. As anyone in the AEC industry can tell you, these costs are increasing due to limited landfill space and higher tipping fees. I was the Environmental

Manager for Skanska USA's Atlanta office when we implemented an environmental management system in order to be certified in ISO 14001, an international environmental standard.

During the first year, Skanska's Atlanta office saved over $270,000 in waste removal costs and diverted thousands of cubic yards of waste from landfills. During the implementation of this system, we encountered some resistance, especially from the guys in the field. They complained that they didn't have time, couldn't train everyone, and didn't have room for recycling dumpsters – the list was endless. What was the source of this resistance? I was at a loss until I began learning about the power of emotional intelligence.

Take a look again at the typical AEC EI profile (Chapter 1) and the relatively low scores in social responsibility and empathy. Low scores in these areas indicate that these workers may have difficulty seeing the global picture, the effect of their actions on others, and the interconnectedness of everyone on the planet, which is essential for embracing these environmental concepts.

This green building trend also relates to teamwork. The United States Green Building Council's LEED® (Leadership in Energy and Environmental Design) program is a certification process for green buildings. It takes a high performing team involving all project stakeholders to deliver such a project and receive the certification. Without this sense of team, these green projects are quite difficult to complete.

I worked on a LEED project where the relationships were difficult. The owner hired a construction manager who pitted the architect and designers against the contractor. If the project did not achieve LEED certification, both the architect and the contractor would have to pay $50,000 in liquidated damages. The owner thought that this was the best way to limit his liability, but in fact, it made the LEED process quite difficult. The process became more about blaming each other and shedding risk instead of working together as a team.

Environmental issues can impact a company's image as well. Skanska, a multi-national Swedish contractor, learned this hard lesson at the Halland Ridge Tunnel project in Hallandsås, Sweden. A subcontractor was using a grout containing acrylamide, which contaminated the local groundwater. In the United States, this may have resulted in a small article in the newspaper, but in Sweden, there was a media frenzy surrounding this story. As a result, Skanska's reputation was badly tarnished. They have since overcome this environmental debacle with a stronger focus on environmental issues. The entire company now has an environmental management system, and each business unit is certified in ISO 14001. This focus on environmental issues has improved their image and led to more business opportunities worldwide.

The green building trend is here to stay, and the demand for green buildings will only increase. If you are entering into this market, you will do well to address these emotional intelligence competencies prior to any technical training. This will give your people the tools they need to be able to understand and implement these green building strategies, improve your organization's image, and capture more of this emerging market. Projects will be better for all stakeholders from owners to designers to contractors to facilities maintenance folks.

Chapter 13

HUMAN RESOURCE PROCESSES

Let's discuss some human resource processes such as hiring, review processes, turnover, training, retention, and succession planning.

Hiring and Recruiting: Current research has determined that a bad hire can cost as much as two to three times their annual salary. And in this current job market post great recession, good hiring practices are vital. Yet most companies continue to make the same hiring mistakes. For someone who makes an annual salary of $80,000, the costs for making a poor hire can run upward to $240,000! Most companies to whom we have talked have insufficient processes in place for recruiting and hiring. These processes consist mainly of impromptu interviews. Few, if any of the managers have been trained in interviewing techniques. The lack of effective hiring processes can be costly.

A leader at a top five contractor here in the United States confided to me that they end up hiring "the best of the worst". Companies can make better decisions by determining what skills are required for each position and whether or not the candidate possesses those skills. A great way to match these skills is by using the EQ-i® 2.0 evaluation. Before, it was difficult to measure soft skills such as empathy and interpersonal relationship skills during the interview process. Now we can measure these traits and make better hiring decisions.

Recently, we received a call from an extended stay hotel company who was interviewing for a mid-level management position. After an initial interview, they had some concern about the candidate's interpersonal skills, and there were indications that this person may be a micromanager. So, they decided to invest in an EQi evaluation. The evaluation showed that the candidate had good interpersonal skills and also showed relatively low flexibility, low self-regard, high problem-solving skills and high reality testing. This profile indicates control/perfectionism, which could manifest itself in the form of micromanaging.

We recommended some behavioral type interview questions to make sure that these areas would not be a problem. To address the flexibility and potential control issues, the company asked, "We value letting our employees stretch themselves in their positions. Can you tell us about a time in your work history where you had to be very flexible and let subordinates do things their own way?" According to the company's managers, using the EI profile was a great way to avoid hiring the wrong person. And companies who avoid making bad hires will save money.

Since the great recession, we are experiencing a workforce crisis. Hiring is ramping up. Most companies are scrambling for talent. They are crisis hiring without any processes in place and will be creating problems for themselves down the road. In addition, if you work on your employees' emotional intelligence and focus on teaching them how to create great relationships, you will be better prepared. The internal relationships will improve your entire business, the external relationships will create new business, and the ongoing relationships will generate future business. In addition, the connections that your employees have will help you to find the best people when you ramp up your hiring.

Review Processes and Retention: Can you remember when people worked for the same company for their entire careers? This is no longer true. It is estimated that Millennials will have ten to fourteen jobs by age 38. A recent article in Engineering News Record discussed the high cost of turnover. Catherine Santee, Senior Vice President of Finance for CH2M Hill stated, "All of us are fighting for talent." Michael Creed, CEO of McKim and Creed added, "We've finally realized we're in the people business."

So what makes people stay with companies for longer periods of time? Of course, there are issues such as compensation and benefits, but if you want to retain great employees, you must look beyond those numbers. In short, if employees feel valued and taken care of, if they are offered ways to develop themselves, their job skills, and their life skills, they will stay with the company longer. Health and wellness is also becoming more and more important to employees. If you can offer ways to keep your employees healthy by offering classes and a comprehensive wellness program, they will be more likely to stay.

Most companies do not give their employees enough ongoing performance management training and very little ongoing feedback and communication. Most organizations in our industry do not have meaningful review processes that discuss career goals, personal goals, and developmental needs, while some companies have no review process in place at all. And those that do have something in place, it's usually an annual check the box meeting with little meaning. Without these reviews, employees tend to feel unappreciated and disengaged.

According to the Gallup Organization, most people leave companies because of poor treatment from their immediate supervisor. Sometimes, this poor treatment manifests itself in a lack of appreciation. If companies improve the EQ of their supervisors and teach them to create a meaningful dialogue with their employees, the employees will feel valued and appreciated, and their level of engagement will increase. According to the ISR, a research and consulting firm, high engagement companies improved their operating incomes by 19.2% while low engagement companies declined 32.7% during the study period.

Managers can engage employees by discussing their developmental needs and helping them to improve. Managers can also use the information for succession planning by determining what competencies are required for future positions, then help the employee to measure and improve them. If employees know there is a plan for their future, they will naturally be more engaged and are more likely to stay put. Some employers use training and development programs to honor and reward their star employees.

If we ignore our employees, if we let them stagnate, if we don't offer them a plan for their careers, we will be faced with ever-rising turnover rates and unproductive, unmotivated, disengaged employees. But if we use emotional intelligence to develop managers and employees, to make them more valuable, and to address personal and professional development issues, they will feel appreciated. They will value the company who provides this type of development and will be much less likely to look elsewhere for employment.

Some companies are using the latest technology and social networking sites to promote this sense of connection and feedback. Employees now can tweet (send a short message) and ask for specific feedback. Or managers can tweet the employees to let them know how they are doing and how they can improve. This can be done daily if necessary. This constant feedback along with praise for doing a good job is essential for keeping employees engaged. It also makes them feel valued.

Succession Planning: One of our clients, an engineering firm, has a succession plan that ensures continuity. The two people directly under the CEO are in line for the CEO's position. These positions are thoughtfully filled with the next leaders of the company. When these two heirs apparent took the EQ-i® 2.0, several areas were identified that they could work on to eventually step into the CEO role someday. This organization realized that the skills these individuals utilize now are not the same skills that they will need to run the company. This kind of evaluation and purposeful development for key positions is essential for good succession planning and successful leadership.

There is a great book called *The Leadership Pipeline*, which clearly defines the skills for each level of career and provides the training to get there. There have been several companies that embraced this process and they have found that as you progress up the career ladder, the skills change from technical skills to people skills. That's where emotional intelligence plays a vital role in growing your future leaders.

Another big issue in the AEC industry is stalled career paths. It happens time and time again. When a technically trained or educated person is adept at managing processes, they are promoted. They keep getting promoted until they are no longer managing processes, but they are managing people. And that is when things tend to go awry. They believe themselves to be intelligent and may have highly developed technical knowledge and expertise. Some even have postgraduate degrees in their fields. So why can't they manage people? This frustration often leads to burnout or even worse, demotion or termination. I've seen it enough times to say that it is a trend, indicating a definite need to teach these potential leaders the "soft skills" needed to break through these career barriers.

Another issue associated with succession planning is filling those middle management positions. Most companies have talented young people and seasoned veterans, but there is a dearth of good, qualified, middle managers. These young people are extremely smart. They are able to figure things out quickly. The thing that is usually missing from these young managers is the maturity and the people skills needed to step into leadership positions. By focusing on their emotional intelligence, we can teach them people skills and transition them into leadership positions in a shorter period of time.

Recently, the CEO for a top 50 contractor asked, "What if these guys don't improve their interpersonal skills? Do we fire them?" The short answer is that we must try to match the skills to the position.

Although we have not found this to be true, if an employee continues to have low scores in interpersonal skills, despite efforts in training and development, you may be able to find a position where these skills are less important, where they don't have as much interaction with key stakeholders. Putting people in the right place to make them more comfortable and productive is essential for increasing overall productivity and the bottom line.

Take a look at the typical Estimator EI profile in Chapter 1. With this typical EI profile, they would need some training to step into a Project Manager role.

Training and Development: Is your company wasting money on training and development? Training, for most companies, is about as effective as rearranging the deck chairs on the Titanic. Daniel Goleman refers to corporate training programs as the "Billion Dollar Mistake". Actually, in the United States, the cost could be much higher than that. According to Training Magazine, in 2017, companies spent $90.6 billion on training. You would think that spending money on training would be a good thing. But is it?

Most training is event based and informational. Participants come to a training event and are given loads of information, usually in the form of a lecture or Power Point presentation. Normally, there is very little follow-up or coaching. The facilitators of these events tell you the following: If you can just take one nugget from today, the class will be worth it. I think this is a copout. I call these training events "three-ring binder" programs.

I'm sure you've attended programs where you listen to an eight-hour lecture with lots of good information and received your three-ring binder or thumb drive with all of the Power Points and documents. And what did you do with that information? Probably put it on a shelf or threw it into a drawer and never looked at it again. Until a year later, when you need the binder for something else or you need the thumb drive to transfer some files. When we attend those types of event based, informational trainings, we tend to forget what we learned and go back to our normal routine in a few days.

There is one other training phenomenon I have seen repeated over and over. And companies waste millions of dollars each year. They will find a book. I call it the "book of the year". Some examples of the book of the year are *Good to Great, Who Moved My Cheese? The One Minute Manager, The Fifth Discipline, The Ideal Team Player, The Five Disfunctions of a Team,* or *The Speed of Trust.*

Don't get me wrong. These are all great books. The company will hire a keynote speaker for their annual managers' meeting, and they will listen to a session on the concepts from the book. They will find their hedgehog or talk about finding new cheese or how to be a better manager. There is no application, no follow-up, no learning, and no behavioral change. In a few weeks, it's back to business as usual, and when the planning committee plans their next company meeting, they decide that the previous book didn't create any changes, so they try to find the next book. The problem is not in the book. The problem is in the application. These companies fall into that old training trap. They think that information and awareness create behavioral change. They don't.

These approaches to training are ineffective to say the least. The Vice President of a Federal bank recently told me of an internal group that had horrible communication, personality conflicts, and rampant gossip. They lacked the ability to function well as a team. When I asked about her assessment of the situation, she told me that they were sending them to a ropes course. Now I have nothing against ropes courses. They can be quite entertaining and may ease the superficial issues of such a dysfunctional group for a short period of time. But the underlying issues are never addressed, much less resolved. The emotional competencies that are contributing to the turmoil are not discussed, and there is no fundamental change. The group members tend to revert back to their old ways within a few short days.

If you take a group of construction folks with the typical AEC emotional intelligence profile, and try to teach them some type of interpersonal skill, they may not have the emotional makeup or the right tools to be able to implement what you are trying to teach them. The wiser strategy is to start with an evaluation of their emotional intelligence. This will not only provide a foundation from which to work, but it will allow you to target specific areas for development. You will have laid the proper foundation to ensure that all future training will be applied in a meaningful way.

You must use the latest neuroscience to develop program content and delivery so that participants will actually apply the information and create behavioral change. Activity-based learning, which is hands on and experiential, is the most effective way to learn. Games are also a great way to learn. Studies have shown that they are not only fun, but very effective learning models. Do your best to use role-plays, applied improvisation, storytelling and discussions in the classroom. Have participants get up and move and do a lot of reflective learning, flipped classroom, and self-directed learning. In addition, it is vital to include coaching and follow-up. Without accountability, it is human nature to set these development strategies aside. Check out the principles in a great book called *Brain Rules* by John Medina. According to this neuroscientist, the following brain rules apply:

- Our brains evolved while moving. You have to get people moving in order for them to learn.

- Emotions more readily create memories that you can recall. Have participants tell lots of stories to reinforce the learning. Jesus taught in parables for a reason. It is easy to remember the lessons.

- Repetition-repeat to learn, learn to repeat. Do many reflective learning exercises throughout your programs and make sure there is continuous follow-up and coaching. Encourage participants to roll this learning into their review processes and meet with accountability partners on a regular basis.

- Sleep is vital to preparing your brain to learn and retain. Encourage proper sleep and nutrition to prepare your brain for learning.

- Stress will prevent you from being able to learn. Teach participants how to relax.

- Use all senses. Although vision is the most developed sense, all senses should be used whenever possible. Participants listen to music and have in depth discussions. They perform hands-on, kinesthetic exercises. They practice mindful eating and drinking. They watch videos and look at other visual media. There are stories about students studying for tests while smelling peppermint. When they sniffed the peppermint during the exam, they recalled much more of the information compared to a control group.

- Curiosity creates a sense of wonder. People will want to learn if you challenge them and increase their curiosity.

Companies can now stop throwing money away on training that is soon forgotten. By using this EI methodology to evaluate, measure, and improve these emotional competencies, and by utilizing ongoing coaching and follow-up, along with experiential learning, companies can create fundamental change from within instead of imparting information that will never be applied.

Chapter 14

FREQUENTLY ASKED QUESTIONS

Isn't this just another one of those personality profiles?

Invariably, several program participants tell us they've already taken all of these kinds of tests and that this is nothing new. Many of them have taken the Myers-Briggs or the DISC test. There are literally thousands of these tests on the market today. Most are based on preferences – you know the types of questions – would you rather read a book or sail a boat? For people with low self-awareness, this can be very informative and fun, but most of these tests are rather limited for detailed, personal development.

For those who are somewhat self-aware, these tests are merely confirmations of what they already know. In fact, the common response is, "Yep, that's me. So what?" It is my belief that personality tests, without some kind of context, are limited in their application to personal development. When you take a personality test, you put yourself in some general state of mind. But the choices that you make on those tests may change based on the circumstances. I may be more of an introvert in my personal life, but at work, I'm an extrovert. So how do I answer those questions? Sometimes I would rather be the center of attention, and sometimes, I would rather be alone. They very rarely capture the true nature of the person. These tests simply can't capture the complexity of a human being.

This approach to development using personality types is very prevalent in the training industry. Participants take a test to find out their "type". Usually there are three other "types". You are either a letter or a color or a number or a quadrant or an animal. Then, they teach you about the other three "types" and how to get along with them. This approach is limited at best and can be dangerous. First of all, human beings are far more complex than a single "type". Second, unless you carry the tests around for everyone to take, it takes empathy to determine what the other person's "type" is. And empathy is not our best emotional competence. In fact, for many groups, it is the lowest score. Third, for some people, this is a real copout. They will stereotype people into whatever "type" they determine and treat them a certain way, which may or may not be correct.

Once you develop your emotional skills, you will be able to deal with any type of person in any situation. You will have the self-awareness to know how you are feeling and how you are being perceived and the empathy skills to know how they are feeling. These situations are dynamic. They can come up in an instant. Isn't it better to have good fundamental emotional competence to work from rather than rely on a set of "rules" for certain "types"?

A construction company I worked for used the DISC profile for all of its employees. DISC is a test that indicates the following personality archetypes:

Dominance tends to be direct and guarded
Influence tends to be direct and open
Steadiness tends to be indirect and open
Conscientiousness tends to be indirect and guarded

As it turned out, 80% of the people in our construction company fell into the Dominance category. What does that tell you? Most people in the construction business have a dominant style. They tend to be direct and guarded. Didn't we know that already?

Myers-Briggs, another personality test whose validity is constantly called into question, indicates the following traits:

Extraversion versus Introversion E or I
Sensing versus Intuition S or N
Thinking versus Feeling T or F
Judging versus Perceiving J or P

When you take the test, you are given a Myers-Briggs Personality Type. But what are you supposed to do with that information? There are some Myers-Briggs modules on teambuilding and how to deal with other Myers-Briggs types, but how do you know the personality type of everyone you encounter? One company made everyone put their Myers-Briggs profile on their coffee cups, but this concept was a miserable failure.

With personality tests, your results rarely change throughout your life, and if they do, it probably has more to do with the context in which you took it. You may shift slightly as you age. The other problem is that there is no clear path to development. If you are an ESFJ, do you want to become an INFT? And how do you do that exactly? What are the development strategies to get you there? There are none. Simply knowing yourself better does not create behavioral change that you need to be able to attain your goals. We say it over and over in our courses: Awareness alone will not change behavior!

The EQ-i® 2.0 is a very different tool and should be used in conjunction with personality tests. It measures specific competencies such as empathy, assertiveness, and problem-solving skills. It is very dynamic and reflects what is going on in your life and work at the time. If you are going through a difficult time, it will be reflected in the scores. This is much more valuable information. It is our experience that if there are behavioral issues, it ALWAYS shows up in their EI profile. Then, you can target specific areas to improve. When you look at that snapshot and where you want to be in the future, it becomes extremely practical. You choose areas to develop, and a detailed development plan is created utilizing specific development strategies. There is practical application, measurement, and improvement. This creates fundamental behavioral shifts. Personality tests alone simply do not do that.

Is there a correlation between emotional intelligence and performance?

I facilitated a program for a top 100 contractor based in the southern United States using emotional intelligence as a foundation for leadership development. After the managers were evaluated, I ranked their interpersonal scores (empathy, social responsibility, and interpersonal relationship skills) from the highest to the lowest. This company had their own ranking system in order to identify their star performers, the ones who contributed most to the success of the company. The astonishing fact was that the company's overall ranking and the ranking of interpersonal skills correlated almost one-to-one. This told us that the managers who had the best interpersonal skills were also the company's stars. They were the managers involved in the most profitable projects who contributed the most to the company's bottom line.

Take a look at a superstar profile:

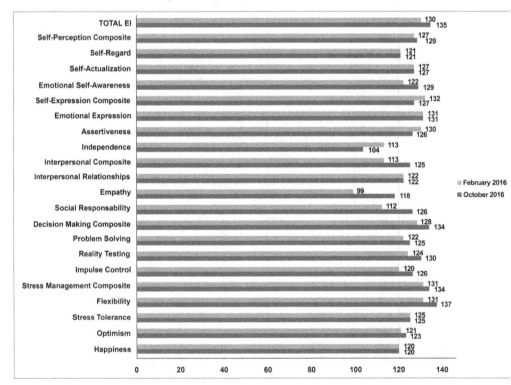

Neha is a very smart woman. She's a Stanford graduate and entered our program as a Project Manager. Note her before scores. She has a fairly balanced profile and the scores are quite high. Many are well into the above average range. Note the relatively lower score in empathy, which is what she chose to work on.

There is a story where the project team (all men) were trying to figure out how to bring precast double tees to the project to build a parking deck. These tees are long, 90′ beams and extremely hard to maneuver using the narrow alleyway entrance to the project. Neha (remember her high independence and assertiveness) proposed that they contact the Georgia DOT and request a lane closure on Georgia 400 to make the pick. They told her that would never work because of their past experience with the Georgia DOT. She left the office, contacted the Georgia DOT, set up a meeting on her own, procured the permit and finished the project on time.

Now take a look at the after scores. She increased her empathy dramatically, which lowered her assertiveness. Her social responsibility also went up along with a decrease in independence. By working on her empathy, she made a very strong profile even stronger by creating even more balance. She became more of a team player and better able to read others. Through this process she was promoted to Senior Project Manager and is now in the process of developing and pursuing new clients in a new region. This is a great example of how a very strong emotional profile can be made even stronger and how emotional profiles can become a predictor of success.

Multi-Health Systems, the owner of the EQ-i® 2.0, has a program called *Star Performer* where companies look at the EI profiles of their star performers for particular departments or positions and determine with statistical accuracy which emotional competencies are essential for high performance. Then it is just a matter of recruiting, hiring, and training for those competencies. The drawback to this approach is in the performance criteria, which must be objective. For sales, performance is objective and clear. For project managers, it is less clear. You may have a high performer that loses $100,000 on a project that would have lost $1 million. Or you may have a low performer that makes $500,000 on a project that was supposed to make $1 million.

Can emotional intelligence be learned?

Seabiscuit was just a broken-down horse incapable of winning until someone saw his potential and developed it through training. It was only then that he became one of the greatest racehorses in the history of racing. The trick is to be able to identify individual potential and develop it with effective techniques. But how do you teach something like empathy? We have developed a methodology targeted for the AEC industry. It was co-developed with Kate Cannon, a pioneer in the field of emotional intelligence.

After the initial EI evaluation and feedback, participants are taken through a half-day program where each participant creates detailed, individual development plans. The participant targets specific competencies based on their future needs and then chooses development strategies from different categories depending on their learning style. They also create plans for mental and physical peak performance that are tied into their emotional plans focusing on nutrition, exercise, and stress management. We utilize many different types of exercises and development ideas and use various media such as books, fables, movies, television, magazines, operas, plays, and websites.

We also emphasize the day-to-day application of this learning and provide inspirational quotes for each competency. In addition, there are many levels of accountability built in. In a group setting, everyone has an accountability partner. They also provide me with accountability partners above them, beside them, below them, family and friends, and clients. After the six-month mark, I call these accountability folks to see if they have seen any changes. We also have the participants do a homework exercise where they meet with their accountability partners and ask them if they have seen any changes. They report their responses back to us. They also have a dialogue with their accountability partners and ask them how they can do better at creating and showing these changes.

These are all powerful ways to keep the learning in the forefront, but the key to this learning is in the follow-up and coaching. We provide 24/7 coaching and follow up for all participants in all programs. They can call us any time with issues related to their development, issues with other people, and situations where they need help. We contact individuals every three or four weeks to check on their progress, offer encouragement, and provide coaching. We also do as many face-to-face coaching sessions during the program as possible. We also send out weekly articles and weekly blogs. Without this individual coaching and follow-up, the participants tend to set aside their development plans. But if they know they will be re-evaluated and that someone will be checking in with them every few weeks, they are much more likely to work on their development plans and create fundamental behavioral change from within. One participant said this about the process, "I thought that people are who they are by their mid-twenties. I definitely feel that people are capable of significant change."

Take a look at the before and after graph for the industry:

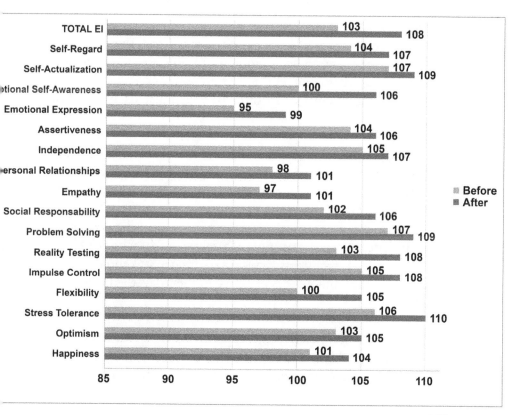

As you can see these emotional skills can be measured and improved. When you see a delta of five points or greater, that is statistically significant. You can clearly see that overall, this group's emotional competence improved (+5). Also, it is a more balanced profile. Note that before, the delta between empathy and assertiveness was 8 points. After, it's only 6 points. Note statistically significant increases (5 points or greater) in emotional self-awareness (+7) and empathy (+5), and a four-point increase in emotional expression, social responsibility, reality testing, and flexibility. Keep in mind, this is a large group. The increases and decreases tend to cancel each other out.

People often ask: How do you teach emotional intelligence competencies? There are hundreds of ways including daily application exercises, long term exercises, movies and television, websites and apps, books and written materials. There is an empathy exercise that is extremely effective. Each participant comes home from work, dismisses the children, turns off the television, sits their spouse down and asks them to talk about their day. The participant cannot solve any of the spouse's problems, offer any suggestions, or make any comments during their monologue. The only thing the participant is supposed to do is try to understand the feelings that the spouse has experienced throughout their day. The only comment the participant can offer is "that must have made you feel…"

After the spouses overcome the initial shock of this, they are quite pleased. In fact, several participants reported a spark of romance after this session. Talk about positive reinforcement for developing your empathy skills! Once the participants can tap into the power of empathy, they are motivated to apply it in the workplace. By truly listening and putting themselves in the shoes of trade partners, owners, architects, and other project stakeholders, they find that they are much more effective in their day-to-day dealings with them.

I love to tell the story of Bryan, a superintendent in his late thirties with an anger problem. He told me that this problem had troubled him since he was young, and that if I could help him find a way to control it, he would be most grateful. This issue showed up in his EQ-i® 2.0. He had low emotional self-awareness along with high assertiveness and low impulse control. His low emotional self-awareness didn't allow him to feel himself getting angry, and eventually, with his low impulse control, it just boiled over.

The first thing Bryan did was work on his emotional self-awareness. He learned to become more aware of where he felt anger in his body and identify it as early as possible. He also worked on basic breathing and meditation techniques along with centering techniques to help with his impulse control.

I gave him a book to read and told him that it may be a little "out there" for him, but to try and find something he could relate to. In the process of reading the book, he found a centering technique that worked for him. He created a focal point by putting a photograph of his two small girls on his mobile phone. When he felt himself getting frustrated (with greater emotional self-awareness, he felt it in his body), he excused himself from the situation, took ten deep breaths, flipped open his phone, and looked at his little girls. This allowed him to decompress and control his anger.

In his words, "Leaving a bad situation, even briefly, has allowed me to not act in anger or impulsively." He improved his emotional management and changed his behavior, making him a more effective leader. With this shift, he has learned to listen more without being so reactive. He told me that the people who work with him have noticed these changes. As he puts it, "Listening, not reacting to people I encounter has led to a more positive approach to my professional life." In addition to improved leadership skills, there has also been an improvement in his mental and physical performance. He is less stressed and better able to handle difficult situations without compromising his health.

Even if the scores from the EQ-i® 2.0 do not increase; there still can be some very useful information for the participant. Annelise, a purchasing manager from Denmark, decided to work on her social responsibility, which was relatively low. Eleven months later, at the end of the program, when she took the EQ-i® 2.0 again, she found that her social responsibility score was even lower. Interestingly enough, her self-actualization, happiness, and optimism had increased dramatically.

When these numbers were discussed, I asked her why she chose to work on social responsibility. She told me that she believed that it was the right thing to do, that she thought her family and friends wanted her to spend more time with them. I asked her if she had spent more time with family and friends in an effort to increase her social responsibility. She replied that she had not. She told me that work had been particularly hectic, and she had been working non-stop since the beginning of the program. She usually worked alone rather than in groups or teams. She also indicated that she felt a little guilty for working so much.

I asked her if she enjoyed working and she responded by saying that it was the most important thing in her life. She loved the challenge and felt that the company needed her during this particularly difficult period, which made her feel valued and important. That was the reason for her significant increases in self-actualization, happiness, and optimism. I suggested that perhaps this second evaluation revealed that during this period in her life, her work, which gave her great joy, was something that she would do well to focus on. In addition, since she worked alone, this way of working did not contribute to increasing her social responsibility. This conversation was a great relief to her. Perhaps all she needed was permission to enjoy her work life without guilt. So, in this case, although the competency she had originally chosen decreased, the results of the second EQ-i® 2.0 gave us some real insights into the direction she wanted for her personal and professional life.

Isn't this just another management fad?

I have given much thought and introspection to this question. As a matter of fact, I considered this possibility when I first started this work. But after seeing the results and seeing the supporting data, the answer to this question is a resounding NO! I've been working with emotional intelligence in the AEC industry since

2000. It is not going away. In fact, neuroscience is verifying what we intuitively know to be true every day.

The shelves are filled with thousands of self-help books for managers. And many of these books contain good information. So, why do management fads come and go like the tides? Because there is a fundamental flaw in their application. They pile generic information on top of generic problems without regard to the individual. No matter how good the information is or how valid the approach, without addressing the fundamental emotional makeup of the individual, the application of this information may never take place.

Most companies agree that communication is essential in the AEC industry. Companies spend millions of dollars on training to give their people better communication skills. But because of the typical EI profiles of most people in the AEC industry, they are often incapable of applying this training. If they have high assertiveness, independence, and self-regard, and low empathy, emotional expression and interpersonal relationship skills, they will likely come across as someone who doesn't express themselves well, doesn't listen, won't ask for other's opinions, and does whatever they think is best regardless of any group input. You can put that person in a communication seminar or buy them books to teach them how to communicate, but it is very probable that they will still be unable to communicate effectively when the seminar is over.

If someone has high reality testing and problem solving along with low flexibility and optimism, they may have issues concerning change. This person will have a very rigid approach to life and work. This person can go to a seminar on change management or read a book like *Who Moved My Cheese?* but his lack of flexibility usually prevents him from truly embracing change. He will have difficulty in the AEC industry because of the constant change, but if his flexibility and optimism are increased, he will be much better able to deal with this issue.

Using emotional intelligence as the foundation for development programs is a different approach. Instead of starting with a particular area of training such as communication or teambuilding, you address the fundamental emotional developmental needs of every individual. Then you address these needs with specific, targeted learning modules. By addressing the emotional competencies first, the participants can develop the emotional makeup to be able to apply the concepts of the learning modules. All future training can be related back to the employees' emotional intelligence development plans, which also make any subsequent company training more effective.

As Lisa Fanto, the Vice President of Human Resources for Holder Construction Company put it, "I've been in and managed corporate education for a long time, and I've seen all of the fads du jour come and go and suffered through many of them. This is the only thing I've seen ever in my career that actually changes lives. I know that sounds dramatic, but it does. It actually changes people. And in order to change the way people manage, you have to change the way they live."

Chapter 15

HOW DO WE GET THERE FROM HERE?

A Step-by-Step Methodology for Improving Emotional Intelligence

"Things do not change; we change".
Henry David Thoreau

People often ask me what percentage of people in our programs actually create lasting changes. My answer is simple. For people that want to create change, it's 100%. For people who don't want to create change, it's 0%.

We have learned many lessons from these programs over the years. We have learned what works and what does not work. We have developed a very good methodology that is highly successful. Here is the step-by-step process.

1. Learn more about emotional intelligence. There are many books on the subject. Discuss the basics and the options.

2. Choose a consultant. Be sure that you choose someone who is certified to administer evaluations and give feedback. It is also important that the consultant understand your business and the way emotional intelligence relates to improving it.

3. Choose an evaluation tool. The EQ-i® 2.0 is an excellent self-assessment tool, but there are several very good tools on the market. MSCEIT® is another instrument that measures EQ. The difference is that MSCEIT® is an ability based EI evaluation instead of a self-assessment. You may choose to do a 360 evaluation where the employee measures his own EQ, and

subordinates, peers, bosses, clients, family, and friends evaluate him as well. We also use a tool called the Symptom Survey to let us know how the body is working based on physical symptoms. We then correlate the emotional and the physical and create development plans for both. You can't separate them. One affects the other. The third evaluation is one called Social Styles™, which gives you a very good idea of how you interact with others and yours and other's communication preferences. This evaluation is based on observable behaviors and has a multi-rater feature so you can see how people are perceiving you and your social style.

4. Start with the top management. Then move on to a group of managers in your company whom you believe will benefit from this type of work. The selection process should be well thought out, and the participants should be given a quick overview of emotional intelligence prior to taking the EQ-i® 2.0.

5. Have participants take the evaluation and receive feedback. Make it clear that these evaluations are confidential and will not be shared with anyone in the company. We emphasize that the EQ-i® 2.0 is a snapshot in time and ask each participant to think about what they need going forward personally and professionally.

6. Have each participant create detailed, integrated development plans. They can create an emotional plan, a physical plan, or a general plan (finances, a hobby, quitting smoking, eating better, life balance), or all three. This preliminary work will give participants a better understanding of themselves, their limitations, and what to work on. We also incorporate peak performance into this discussion and show participants the mind-body link between the emotional and the physical and how they affect each other.

    Do some initial exercises to set a baseline. One is called the Four Quadrants (in Appendix A: Resources). You can also download the Toolbox Safety Topics by visiting *www.brentdarnell.com/resources*. Participants divide a piece of flip chart paper into four quadrants and label them family, work, personal, and hopes/dreams/aspirations. They also list the perfect project outcome for them. At the top, they put their name and their favorite piece of music. We create a playlist from everyone's music and play it often during the program. At the bottom, they put some of their challenges on the project and personally and professionally. This is a great exercise. It breaks down barriers and creates a lot of emotional threads among the participants. This information is kept for each individual forever so they can check in occasionally to see what has changed.

Also have them write a letter to themselves dated the last day of the program that lists all of their accomplishments that they have attained as a result of the program. This future diary plants all of their accomplishments in their subconscious so that even if they aren't thinking about them consciously, they are still working on them. Recently, participants have opted to make a mind movie, which is a visual future diary. There is a website that can facilitate this process, and you can even post your movie on You Tube. This work at the subconscious level is very powerful. We use relaxation, visualization, and self-hypnotism to change those old tapes in your head so that you can achieve all that you want to achieve. This focus on the subconscious level facilitates the creation of new neural pathways in the emotional part of your brain. In fact, in a recent study at a management institute in India, they found that people who regularly practiced yoga and meditation had higher levels of emotional intelligence.

7. Determine the group scores and address any group developmental needs. For the AEC industry, these needs usually lie in the area of interpersonal skills and emotional self-awareness. Reinforce this emotional intelligence learning process with learning modules such as communication skills, relationships skills, teambuilding, negotiation skills, coaching, and motivation. Teach the group about stress management and time management. These learning modules may also include areas specific to the company or group such as business strategies and vision. Insist on programs that are customized to

each individual, to each group, and to your company. And with minimal lecture and self-directed, experiential learning, each program can be truly unique.

8. Spread out the learning process. This type of emotional learning takes place in a different part of the brain than cognitive learning. It's not like solving a problem. It is more like learning a language or learning to play a musical instrument. It takes repetition and internalization over a longer period of time. We recommend a minimum of nine months to one year. In our experience, after the initial excitement of starting a program wears off, there is always a lull. After continuous follow-up and coaching, this lull is overcome and progress is made. We generally start to see behavioral shifts at the four-to-five-month mark. After nine months, this behavioral shift is fairly permanent. Then, give the program a few extra months just to be sure that the transformation is permanent.

9. Create an atmosphere of learning, not an atmosphere of training. We use the latest studies in neuroscience that tells us how people learn and retain information. When possible, mobile phones are turned on for the day or used in the learning process. We involve as many of the senses as possible during the learning process. We utilize reflective learning continually because repetition creates retention. We get people out of their seats as much as possible because we learn better when our bodies are moving and use experiential, activity-based learning, applied improvisation, storytelling, and gamification of learning.

10. Build in accountability. Without it, there is less focus on learning and less behavioral change. Build in as much accountability as you can. Ask participants to roll this work into their review process. Ask them to involve as many people in their journey as possible. We require a list of accountability folks who are above them, beside them, below them, a family or friend, and a client or someone outside of their company. After six months, we call every one of these accountability partners and ask them if they are seeing any changes in the participant. We also have

the participants meet with their accountability folks and report their responses to us.

11. Coach the participants during the learning process. This ongoing coaching will reinforce the learning and hold the participants accountable for implementing their development plans. Without coaching and follow-up, there is little change. See the following graph. I worked with a group of higher-level executives for one day to show them the process that their direct reports were experiencing. They took the EQ-i® 2.0, received feedback, and created detailed development plans. They had the best intentions of carrying those plans out. Then I went away.

There was no coaching or follow-up. Fast forward three years. Because the most common comment we get from participants is, "My boss needs to take this course," these same guys ended up in a full-blown course with coaching and follow-up. They re-took the EQ-i® 2.0. Look at the scores between the first and second EQi 2.0 in the following graph.

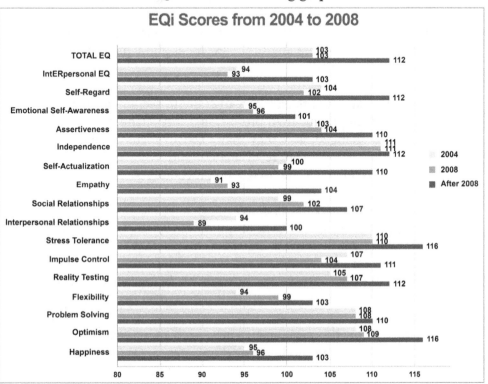

175

Basically, nothing changed. The only two statistically significant changes (5 points or more) were flexibility, which went up by five and interpersonal relationships, which went down by five. After the yearlong course, take a look at the results on the third EQ-i® 2.0. There were statistically significant increases in many areas. Their behaviors had definitely changed.

12. Have the participants retake the EQ-i® 2.0 evaluation and receive feedback. Discuss the changes in the scores and what they mean as well as the individual's EI development plan and behavioral changes.

13. Provide a wrap-up session where participants discuss their before and after scores and what they mean in terms of their development. Celebrate the accomplishments and analyze the shortfalls, then end with a discussion of how to create lifelong learning. Re-evaluate the development plans and modify accordingly. We check in with our four quadrants to see what has changed. They read the letters that they wrote to themselves. We watch the mind movie. Then, we take all of this into account, reflect on it, ask ourselves where we want to go from here, then create development plans going forward filled with accountability. They also create new letters to self or mind movies to incorporate all of the new focus and what they want to accomplish in the coming year.

14. Have the participants check in annually to see where they are in their development. Their professional and personal situations may have changed, and they may need to focus on different areas. They should be re-evaluated and receive individual feedback as a part of the follow-up procedure.

    Without the coaching and follow-up and accountability, the participants will revert back to old behaviors, especially under times of stress. It is vital that participants check in annually and that companies create ways to hold them accountable. Otherwise, the return on investment in training can be diminished.

15. At this point, the participants may need more coaching and reinforced learning modules to address new areas of learning.

16. For individuals, you can start on your journey to improve your emotional intelligence today. The first step is to take the EQ-i® 2.0 and receive feedback. The next step is to work through our EI Roadmap workbook and create development plans.

LESSONS LEARNED: There are several errors that companies have made with regard to this emotional intelligence work. In order to avoid these mistakes, be aware of the following:

1. It is a good idea to take top managers through this type of evaluation and training first. Make sure this work is aligned with the company vision and values. We had one participant who told his boss he was working on empathy. His boss replied, "No you're not." His boss thought that empathy equated to weakness and this company was not going to show weakness. You don't want participants to return to their jobs to find resistance to these emotional intelligence concepts. If they are working to improve their interpersonal skills while senior managers are neglecting theirs, they will be frustrated. Senior management must know what this work is and support it fully.

   I talked to one company that I thought would be a good fit for this type of work. They had a daycare center in their offices. When I gave my pitch to the HR manager, he told me that he didn't think the company would embrace this emotional intelligence work. I asked him about the daycare center, and he told me that the only reason they had a daycare center was because it encouraged the employees to work longer hours. With this type of company value (work extremely hard until you have a heart attack and die) emotional intelligence simply won't work.

2. Build in as much accountability as possible. You can't have too much. For each class, there are accountability partners in the class. We also ask for accountability partners above them, beside them, below them, a client, and a family/friend. We tell

them that we are going to call these folks after six months to see if they are noticing any changes. Make sure they know that you will be following up with them and their accountability folks throughout the program.

3. Be sure to include follow-up and coaching in the program. When there is no follow-up, participants treat the program as another one of those training programs that wastes their time and yields little practical results. When you work with each individual to create a development plan, coach them through it, and follow-up with a second evaluation and interview, it encourages accountability and gives the program credibility. And when the participants know there will be follow-up, they are much more likely to work on their plans and create fundamental behavioral change from within.

4. Don't be discouraged if all of the participants don't embrace this work. It takes some time to win the skeptical construction folks over, but in the end, nearly all embrace this work and create that fundamental change. There will be some who will never value emotional intelligence work. In our experience, this is less than 5% of the participants. But even those who don't participate fully seem to get something out of the program and find at least one thing that helps them in their life and career.

5. Make sure that the style of teaching is effective for the group. We use a maximum of 20% lecture and we don't use Power Point at all. We use Prezi, which is more visually interesting. The other 80% is activity-based learning, which is experiential and self-directed, filled with improvisation and gamification. Use the latest neuroscience studies on learning and retention. Be sure to incorporate the company's business objectives and make sure the learning is practical and applicable.

6. Make sure to have reunions occasionally to check in. This could be annual or every two years. It doesn't have to be elaborate. Have everyone take the evaluations and meet for a half day of reflection, goal setting and plan creation. The questions are

where am I now? (evaluation results, current state, what has changed?), where do I want to be? (future goals), and how do I get there? (plans)

7. Many training companies are repackaging their canned training programs and referring to them as programs on "emotional intelligence." Let the buyer beware. All of our work is specifically designed for the AEC industry using validated instruments and proven learning methods.

Chapter 16

THE TOTAL LEADERSHIP PROGRAM
AND ONLINE LEARNING

We have taken this mind/body connection to the next level. We have created a program called the Total Leadership Program where we combine mental and physical peak performance with emotional intelligence. We see tangible correlations between the physical evaluation and the emotional evaluation. And when we focused on both, our results took a quantum leap.

This program grew organically. We always give the participants the option of working on something besides emotional intelligence. Keep in mind, many of the groups we work with are filled with middle-aged men. Over 90% of them chose health. They wanted to lose weight, quit smoking, eat better, exercise more, and reduce their stress.

We have created a customized peak performance program for these construction folks. That way, we can get a baseline and see if the program has had a positive effect on their level of performance both from a physical and mental standpoint.

We are seeing patterns in typical physical profiles and how they match the EQ-i® 2.0 profiles. For instance, whenever we see low impulse control and high assertiveness (frustration, impatience, and anger), we now ask the person if they have a poor diet and eat a lot of carbohydrates and sugar. And many of them have said yes. One of the participants told us he never realized how much diet and exercise affected his emotional state and problem-solving capability. Another participant told us that since she has cut out sugar during her day, her problem-solving capacity has increased tremendously. She told us that toward the end of the program, she received an out of sequence bonus, a raise, and a promotion. She also improved her mental and physical performance dramatically.

A very large, multi-national contractor sent two people to our last Total Leadership Program. They told them that they were sending them to this program to make some changes or be fired. I told the HR person that we don't fix people, but we would certainly do our best. At the end of the program, both participants not only survived a round of over 300 layoffs in their West Coast offices, but one was promoted. In addition, they both changed their lives for the better. They had better relationships with family members, were better able to cope with stress, and were generally much happier. The HR person who sent these people told us, "You saved two very valuable employees. And you can bet that if they are still working with us, they are "A" players."

Another company, a medium sized glass installation company, brought ten participants because they saw the value of the program from the very beginning. Many of these participants were high school educated, blue-collar workers, and they made huge changes in their lives and work.

One of our biggest successes has been Jacobsen Construction in Salt Lake City. They wanted to create a cultural shift in the company, so they took every person through our Total Leadership Program, which is a year-long program, and a large commitment of time, energy, and resources. From the CEO down to the Foreman level, every person went through this training. It took four years. And the change in the company was remarkable. They went from a fairly stodgy, 90-year-old, very solid company to a company that is driven by relationships. Their new tag line is "making life better".

Matt Rich, Vice President at Jacobsen Construction, said, "Having Brent work with our company changed our organization from the inside out. He helped us establish a vocabulary across our organization that enabled seasoned (and hardened) superintendents to relate better to their teams and their clients. Brent showed our people that it's okay to have feelings and even more okay to respect other people's feelings. We still have a lot of work to do but we now have individual plans to help us become better employees and better people."

This program changes people's lives and transforms companies. If you want more information, visit *www.brentdarnell.com*.

We have recently partnered with CMAA to put all of these courses on their learning platform. You can visit brentdarnell.com and click on the online courses tab for more information and to try out some sample courses. All courses are eligible for continuing education credits.

Chapter 17

FINAL THOUGHTS

My wife and I were in Amsterdam and took in a concert at a very famous concert hall called the Consertgebouw. We heard Nigel Kennedy, a brilliant violinist, but quite different from any violinist we had seen before. He wore his hair in a spiky Mohawk. He wore boots and a silk coat unlike the members in the orchestra, who all had white ties and tails. The first thing he did was take down the velvet ropes that separated the audience from the orchestra. With a great flourish, he said, "Now we are united!"

During the concert, he acted more like a rock and roll star than a classical violinist. He rocked back and forth with orchestra members and danced around the stage. At one point, he walked off stage while playing and came back on kicking a soccer ball. Continuing to play, he kicked the ball out into the audience. It was a delight watching his passion and his great musical ability.

At the end of the concert, I leaned over to my wife and said, "I want to be that guy. I want to be that weird guy who is passionate about what he does and gets great results even though people look at him as someone who is a little bit out there." She thought a minute and said, "You teach emotional intelligence, yoga, and meditation to contractors. I think you are that guy."

I love this industry and am proud to be an engineer. I remember as a kid going to the jobsite on Saturdays with my Dad. This was before OSHA of course. My brothers and I would ride up in the buck hoist and run wild on the floors of the high rise inching our way toward the edge of the building where the only thing that stood between us and certain death was a couple of thin steel cables. It was exhilarating. I was in awe that my dad could be a part of this. And every time we drove past anything that dad worked on, we

G. Brent Darnell

always said, "That's Dad's building" or "Dad built that building." There was always a sense of great pride.

I understand the reluctance of the people in the AEC industry to embrace this work because it is outside of their comfort zones. I probably won't grow a Mohawk, but I will continue this work with passion and enthusiasm because I have seen emotional intelligence change people's lives and transform companies.

We have been grappling with these AEC industry problems for decades, perhaps centuries. Isn't it time we focused on the root causes of these problems and addressed them head on? When I saw the connection between the typical emotional intelligence profiles and the major industry problems, I felt like Marlon Brando's character, Walter Kurtz, in the movie *Apocalypse Now*. I had this sudden insight "like a diamond in the middle of my forehead."

If companies begin to realize that people are their most precious resource, if they are willing to take a chance and use this incredible tool called emotional intelligence, they will begin to hire the right people, nurture them, promote their personal development, give them direction for their careers, plan for succession, decrease turnover rates, and increase retention. In addition, this will facilitate increased customer service, teamwork, and productivity. In turn, safety incidents, stress, and burnout will decrease. Their employees will be healthier, happier, and more productive.

Companies that embrace this work will improve the industry image so that young people will flock to our ranks, and our sons and daughters will carry on this proud tradition of contracting. What's the alternative? If we let things continue as they are, the industry may be in trouble. Our inaction could cripple construction, but our focus on people will lead us to lasting solutions.

These types of problems are not limited to the AEC industry. In fact, most industries are encountering these issues. All industries can benefit from this EI methodology by focusing more on the human factor. When you get right down to it, business is all about

186

people. And people are all about emotional intelligence. Let's put the people dimension back into our business. Let's make the phrase "people are our most important asset" more than just a slogan. Your employees are your only long-term, competitive advantage. Companies must pay attention to the people profit connection. Because if companies take care of their people, people will take care of their companies, projects will be more successful, and profits will soar.

RESOURCES AND OTHER BOOKS

Other resources by G. Brent Darnell:

The Tough Guy Survival Kit (includes Communication and Presentation Skills, Relationship Skills, and Stress Management, Time Management, and Life Balance:

The Tao of Emotional Intelligence: 82 Ways to Improve Your Social Competence:

The Primal Safety Coloring Book:

Big Mama's Country Cookbook: Recipes from the True South:

Meditation CD with 3 tracks of music and four guided meditations.

The Tao of Emotional Intelligence App.

All books are available as paperback or e-books on all online booksellers. The meditation CD is available on CD Baby. The App is available on Android and Apple. Please visit the online store at www.brentdarnell.com for links to all resources.

BIOGRAPHY AND CONTACT INFORMATION

Brent Darnell is a mechanical engineer by education, is a leading authority on emotional intelligence and is a pioneer of its use in the AEC industry. Brent has helped to improve the social competence and mental, physical, and emotional performance of thousands of people working with over 200 companies in more than 20 countries around the world. There is constant demand for him to deliver speeches and train others using his comprehensive and unique approach that leads to lasting behavioral transformation.

An engineer, author, actor, playwright, and musician, Brent gives presentations that are insightful, perceptive, and wildly entertaining. The AEC industry has embraced his work, and many top companies like Beck, Clark, Granite, Kiewit, Caddell, Batson-Cook, Brasfield & Gorrie, INPO, S&ME, Langan Engineers, Geotechnical Services, Inc, Pinkerton & Laws, Randall Paulson, Manhattan, Lyles, Newcomb & Boyd, Guarantee Electric, Hardin, McCarthy, Heery, Jacobsen, Cousins Properties, WS Nielsen, Balfour Beatty, and Skanska, have utilized his methods for their managers. He has also worked with the CMAA, the COAA, CII, CURT, DBIA, ASFE, the Associated General Contractors, and the Associated Builders and Contractors. In addition, he is an adjunct professor at Auburn, Virginia Tech, University of Cincinnati, and Northwestern, teaching people skills to their technical students.

Brent believes a person's emotional intelligence is one of the most important predictors of ultimate success for individuals and companies, and his proven program creates fundamental behavioral shifts in employees, improving their performance and increasing the company's bottom line. Brent is a graduate of the Georgia Institute of Technology and lives in Atlanta.

If you wish to contact Brent Darnell concerning this emotional intelligence work, please visit *www.brentdarnell.com*.

You may also email him at *brent@brentdarnell.com* or drop him a line at 1940 The Exchange, Suite 100, Atlanta, GA 30339 USA

APPENDIX A: RESOURCES

GHYST EMOTIONAL INTELLIGENCE TEST AND WORKBOOK

Name: **DAMON IHLER**   Date: **1-19-22**

Work your way through the test, then read through the interpretive guidelines for the various typical profiles and pairings of competencies. Then, read through how these typical profiles affect the different areas of your life and work.

	Emotional and Social Skills	STRONGLY AGREE(SA)	AGREE(A)	NEUTRAL(N)	DISAGREE(D)	STRONGLY DISAGREE(SD)
	Point Value	5	4	3	2	1
1	I have a healthy level of self--respect.		X			
2	I'm comfortable with my general appearance.				X	
3	If someone criticizes me, I'm able to put their feedback into perspective and keep my emotional balance.			X		
4	I make it a habit to take time for personal and professional development.			X		
5	My plans for the future are motivating and energizing.			X		
6	It's easy for me to stay active doing things that I find most fulfilling.		X			
7	My emotional life is rich and varied.			X		
8	I'm in touch with the way I feel in most situations.			X		
9	I'm seldom, if ever, "hijacked" or caught off guard by my emotional responses to situations.			X		
10	I easily express my feelings.				X	
11	I enjoy showing my feelings to others.				X	
12	People tell me they always know how I feel about things.			X		
13	I am able to express my needs and opinions to others.			X		
14	I let others know when I believe they are ignoring my rights in a situation.			X		

	Emotional and Social Skills	STRONGLY AGREE(SA)	AGREE(A)	NEUTRAL(N)	DISAGREE(D)	STRONGLY DISAGREE(SD)
15	I believe that expressing my honest opinion is important in maintaining good relationships.			X		
16	I prefer to make my own decisions.		X			
17	When working alone, I maintain a sure sense of purpose and directions.	X				
18	When working with others, I take the initiative on independent projects.		X			
19	I am comfortable sharing my deep feelings with good friends.			X		
20	My life is enriched by family and close friends.			X		
21	Others feel comfortable confiding in me.			X		
22	I'm good at discerning the way other people perceive their situations, even if different from mine.			X		
23	I easily tune into the feelings of others around me in order to assess the 'emotional climate' of any group.				X	
24	I appreciate it when people treat others with respect and kindness.		X			
25	Helping others outside my immediate family and group of friends is important to me.			X		
26	I impress others as dependable and reliable.			X		
27	It's not in my nature to take advantage of others.			X		
28	When confronted by a new challenge, I find it easy to decide on the best course of action.	X				
29	Even if it takes a long time to deal with a problem, I rarely get discouraged and give up.	X				
30	Even with an overload of information about all the options, I can still make the tough decisions.	X				
31	I'm aware of how my thoughts and beliefs impact my evaluation of circumstances.			X		
32	I learn about different aspects of any issue or problem before taking action.		X			
33	I like to double check my facts to ensure the accuracy of assumptions.		X			
34	I'm not quick to anger or hot--headed.			X		

	Emotional and Social Skills	STRONGLY AGREE(SA)	AGREE(A)	NEUTRAL(N)	DISAGREE(D)	STRONGLY DISAGREE(SD)
35	I am steady, patient and focused in achieving goals.	X				
36	I don't give in easily to temptations or distractions.		X			
37	It's my nature to remain balanced and calm even when things don't go as planned.		X			
38	Others tell me that I deal well with change.			X		
39	I am energized by the excitement, even the uncertainty, of beginning a new project.			X		
40	I usually calm down quickly after a crises has passed.			X		
41	I seldom get annoyed or stressed out by events.			X	X	
42	People look to me for calm assurance and guidance when things get tough.			X		
43	I move forward with confidence despite setbacks.	X				
44	I am confident about my ability to handle the unexpected.	X				
45	In my experience, disappointments, in the longer term, are just stepping stones to success in disguise.				X	
46	I'm an upbeat person who enjoys life.				X	
47	People consider me uplifting and fun.				X	
48	I'm seldom, if ever, depressed or 'down' about things.				X	

DIRECTIONS

For each competence below, go to the statements listed and add up your total results for those three statements. **For each 3-statement competency:**

- If you scored **3-9 total**, this is probably an area that needs improvement.
- If you scored **10-11 total**, your score is better, but still indicates you'd likely benefit from improvement.
- If you scored **12-13 total**, you are probably in the average range.
- If you scored **14-15 total**, you are probably above average in this area.

Often the most revealing aspect of this assessment is the degrees of difference between different scores, an amazingly helpful indicator of performance and behavior. Graph your results on the graph page.

SELF-PERCEPTION

Self-Regard (Statements 1-3) is respecting oneself while understanding and accepting one's strengths and weaknesses. Self-regard is often associated with feelings of inner strength and self-confidence.

Total points: _____9_____

Self-Actualization (Statements 4-6) is the willingness to persistently try to improve oneself and engage in the pursuit of personally relevant and meaningful objectives that lead to a rich and enjoyable life.

Total points: _____10_____

Emotional Self-Awareness (Statements 7-9) includes recognizing and understanding one's own emotions. This includes the ability to differentiate between subtleties in one's own emotions while understanding the cause of these emotions and the impact they have on the thoughts and actions of oneself and others.

Total points: _____9_____

SELF EXPRESSION

Emotional Expression (Statements 10-12) is openly expressing one's feelings verbally and non-verbally.

Total points: _____7_____

Assertiveness (Statements 13-15) involves communicating feelings, beliefs, and thoughts openly, and defending personal rights and values in a socially acceptable, non-offensive, and non-destructive manner.

Total points: _____9_____

Independence (Statements 16-18) is the ability to be self-directed and free of emotional dependency on others. Decision-making, planning, and daily tasks are completed autonomously.

Total points: _____ 13 _____

INTERPERSONAL

Interpersonal Relationships (Statements 19-21) refers to the skill of developing and maintaining mutually satisfying relationships that are characterized by trust and compassion.

Total points: _____ 9 _____

Empathy (Statements 22-24) is recognizing, understanding, and appreciating how other people feel. Empathy involves being able to articulate your understanding of another's perspective and behaving in a way that respects the feelings of others.

Total points: _____ 9 _____

Social Responsibility (Statements 25-27) is willingly contributing to society, to one's social groups, and generally to the welfare of others. Social Responsibility involves acting responsibly, having social consciousness, and showing concern for the greater community.

Total points: _____ 9 _____

DECISION MAKING

Problem Solving (Statements 28-30) is the ability to find solutions to problems in situations where emotions are involved. Problem solving includes the ability to understand how emotions impact decision making.

Total points: _____ 12 _____

Reality Testing (Statements 31-33) is the capacity to remain objective by seeing things as they really are. This capacity involves recognizing when emotions or personal bias can cause one to be less objective.

Total points: _____11_____

Impulse Control (Statements 34-36) is the ability to resist or delay an impulse, drive, or temptation to act. It involves avoiding rash behaviors and decision making. Total points: _____10_____

STRESS MANAGEMENT

Flexibility (Statements 37-39) is adapting emotions, thoughts, and behaviors to unfamiliar, unpredictable, and dynamic circumstances or ideas.

Total points: _____9_____

Stress Tolerance (Statements 40-42) involves coping with stressful or difficult situations and believing that one can manage or influence situations in a positive manner.

Total points: _____9_____

Optimism (Statements 43-45) is an indicator of one's positive attitude and outlook on life. It includes remaining hopeful and resilient, despite occasional setbacks.

Total points: _____11_____

WELL BEING INDICATOR

Happiness (Statements 46-48) is the ability to feel satisfied with one's life, to enjoy oneself and others, and to have fun.

Total points: _____9_____

Note: Although this evaluation may give an indication of areas which need improvement, it should not be used for in-depth, personal development. In order to do that, we recommend that you take the Emotional Quotient Inventory (EQ-i) 2.0, the validated and most widely-used emotional intelligence evaluation in the world. You can then obtain feedback on your results from a qualified, certified emotional intelligence professional. Visit our website and online store for more information.

GRAPHING YOUR RESULTS FOR ANALYSIS / DISCUSSION

3   4   5   6   7   8   9   10   11   12   13   14   15

SELF-PERCEPTION
Self-Regard _____ 9   L
Self- Actualization _____ 10
Emotional Self-Awareness _____ 9

SELF-EXPRESSION
Emotional Expression _____ 7   L
Assertiveness _____ 9
Independence _____ 13

INTERPERSONAL
Interpersonal Relationships _____ 9   L
Empathy _____ 9   L
Social Responsibility _____ 9

DECISION MAKING
Problem Solving _____ 12
Reality Testing _____ 11
Impulse Control _____ 10

STRESS MANAGEMENT
Flexibility _____ 9
Stress Tolerance _____ 9
Optimism _____ 11

WELL BEING INDICATOR
Happiness _____ 9

INTERPRETIVE GUIDELINES

It is desirable to have a balanced profile. Avoid the trap of thinking that a high number is good and a low number is bad. Any strength

197

taken to the extreme may become a weakness, especially if the balancing competency is low. For example: assertiveness is a great leadership skill, but if it is high and empathy is low, you may be perceived as someone who doesn't listen, doesn't ask for input or opinions, and doesn't understand others. Look at the highs and lows of your EI profile. Put an "h" beside your three highest scores and an "l" beside your three lowest scores. Do you have any of the characteristics listed for the following highs and lows?

SELF PERCEPTION COMPOSITE

SELF-REGARD
High: Arrogant, full of yourself.
Low: Shy, lack confidence.

SELF-ACTUALIZATION
High: Have a clear plan for your future, feel good about the direction of your life.
Low: No plan, aimless, no clear vision for future, unhappy in present situation, you may see no way out.

EMOTIONAL SELF AWARENESS
High: Overly sensitive to comments, to others, and possibly to your environment.
Low: Unaware of others, your surroundings, and even your body, you "check out" often.

SELF EXPRESSION COMPOSITE

EMOTIONAL EXPRESSION
High: Easy to win the trust of those who appreciate exuberant expressiveness, though may alienate those who are more reserved.
Low: The opposite: more likely to fail to connect with those who are expressive - but generally better received by emotionally reserved types.

ASSERTIVENESS
High: Bowl people over, don't take into account others' feelings or input - often perceived as aggressive.
Low: Don't speak what is on your mind, don't stand up for yourself, aren't clear in setting expectations or declaring own needs.

INDEPENDENCE
High: Would rather work alone and be alone, not comfortable in groups or teams or social settings.
Low: Dependent on others for self worth, would rather be told what to do, thrive in groups and teams.

INTERPERSONAL COMPOSITE

INTERPERSONAL RELATIONSHIPS
High: Gregarious, have a lot of friends, create instant rapport, stay in touch.
Low: Uncomfortable in social settings and meeting new people, do not stay in touch, may come across as a wallflower.

EMPATHY
High: Very sensitive to the needs of others and their feelings.
Low: Oblivious to others and their needs and feelings.

SOCIAL RESPONSIBILITY
High: Great team member, good neighbor, joiner, like to interact with groups, very social.
Low: You do not do well in groups or teams, not social; don't like to be a member of groups.

DECISION MAKING COMPOSITE

PROBLEM SOLVING
High: Able to arrive at workable solutions to problems quickly and understand how emotions can affect problem solving.
Low: You struggle with defining problems and arriving at solutions and are often overwhelmed emotionally by the problem-solving process.

REALITY TESTING
High: You see things as they really are despite emotions surrounding the situation.
Low: See all of the possibilities, do not investigate or reflect on the specific facts of a situation, live in a world where objective reality is unclear.

IMPULSE CONTROL
High: 'Paralysis of analysis,' over-thinks things, won't pull the trigger.
Low: You may have compulsive or addictive behavior such as eating, drinking, gambling, smoking, sex, spending, talking, etc., in which there is a consistent 'hijacking' of your long-term best interests - resulting in possible profound physical as well as emotional effects.

STRESS MANAGEMENT COMPOSITE

FLEXIBILITY
High: Trouble saying no, take on too much, float from one thing to the next, trouble finishing things.
Low: Very rigid in your approach to things, want to maintain control.

STRESS TOLERANCE
High: Have the ability to handle a lot of stress, good coping skills. Note: We have found that some people with very high stress tolerance may first start to show physical signs of stress like fatigue, headaches or other pains, stomach issues, trouble sleeping, irritability, diminished sex drive, lowered immune response, and depression.
Low: Cluttered, harried, hurried, reactive, unable to stay on top of things, probably have symptoms of stress, feel overwhelmed.

OPTIMISM
High: You consistently see your future as bright and sunny, sometimes to your own detriment. - Glass half full.
Low: The curmudgeon who always looks on the dismal side of life. - Glass half empty.

WELL BEING INDICATOR

HAPPINESS:
High: Shiny, happy person who always seems to be in a good mood and full of joy.
Low: Always seem down and out, life is not fun, you find no joy,

INTERPRETING YOUR HIGH-LOW SCORE DIFFERENCES

Again, the most revealing aspect of this assessment is often the degree of difference between scores. These differences are relative. The relative scores of one competence to another is often an excellent indicator of behavior and performance. Any strength taken to extreme can become a weakness, especially if the balancing emotional competence is low. For example, reality testing is a great decision-making skill, but if it is high and flexibility is low, a person may come across as overly controlling. It is always good to have balance in your profile. For the Ghyst EI Test, a difference of even one point can be significant.

Take a look at your Ghyst EI graph. Put an "H" by the four highest scores and an "L" by the four lowest scores. If you have more than 4, choose the ones most relevant/significant to you.

Look for the following competencies. If you see these relative emotional highs and lows, ESPECIALLY the underlined competencies, you may have the

ALPHA PROFILE:

High: <u>assertiveness</u>, self-regard, and/or independence

Low: <u>empathy</u>, self-awareness, social responsibility, interpersonal relationships, impulse control, emotional expression, flexibility

Take a special look at assertiveness and empathy. These are the main indicators of this profile. If you have the other highs and lows as well, it means that it is highly likely that you have this profile.

Note: If you see a difference of 2 to 3 points on the Ghyst EI evaluation, you may be perceived as abrasive, abrupt, and without tact. You likely don't listen well, don't ask for opinions or input from others, and tend to take charge or take over. If coupled with high self-regard, you may be seen as arrogant. At its most extreme, these ultra alphas can be seen as aggressive, abusive, or bullying.

Alpha Strengths: Strong personality, driver, gets things done, results driven, high performer.

How does this Alpha Profile affect the following?:

Time Management: You may take on way too much because you don't think anyone can do it as well as you can. You may have trouble delegating.

Relationships: Doesn't listen, doesn't ask for opinions or input from others. Takes charge, takes over. If coupled with high self-regard, may be seen as arrogant.

Team Interaction: Has a tendency to take over and not work in a collaborative way.

Communication: Poor listening skills. Lack of understanding of others and their needs.

Presentation Skills: Usually good presenters, but lower empathy prevents a connection with the audience and understanding what they want.

Stress Management: Alphas are frequently stressed and hurried. They rarely take the time for themselves or build in daily reflection and recovery time.

Things to Work On: Empathy is a big key for alphas. By tuning in more to the needs of others, you create more intimate connections with others, which will help with your success both personally and professionally.

Look for the following competencies. If you see these relative emotional highs and lows, ESPECIALLY the underlined competencies, you may have the

SELF-SACRIFICE PROFILE:

High: <u>empathy</u>, self-awareness, interpersonal relationships, social responsibility, flexibility

Low: <u>assertiveness</u>, independence, emotional expression, stress tolerance, self-regard, problem solving

Take a special look at assertiveness and empathy. These are the main indicators of this profile. If you have the other highs and lows as well, it means that it is highly likely that you have this profile.

Self-Sacrifice Strengths: Great team player, very helpful to others, good with people.

How does this Self-Sacrifice Profile affect the following?:

Time Management: Because you may not set proper limits and boundaries and are reluctant to say no, you will likely take on too much and be pulled into other people's agendas. This adds to stress levels and your work suffers.

Relationships: You may have scored lower in relationship skills because your relationships may not be mutually satisfying. You may give more than you get. Self-sacrificers think that when they start setting better limits and boundaries, that people won't like them anymore. The opposite is true. These limits create clear expectations and communication.

Team Interaction: You are a great team member, but you may not speak up and contribute your ideas.

Communication: Because you may be reluctant to say what you are thinking and feeling, there may be miscommunications. You may overpromise and under-deliver because you don't want to say no.

Presentation Skills: You may be reluctant to "put yourself out there" and connect with the audience.

Stress Management: Because you say yes a lot and don't set limits, you will likely take on too much and be overwhelmed much of the time. Stress levels stay high.

Things to Work On: Assertiveness is the key to this profile. Be clear in your communications. Set better limits and boundaries. Begin each day with YOUR list of things to accomplish and don't be pulled off track by others. Have times when your door is closed. When these communications are clear, there is a deeper level of understanding from the people in your life and work. Reduce carbohydrates and sugar and always defer a decision. If someone asks if you can help, tell them that you will let them know in an hour or tomorrow. Then, you will have time to formulate a response. You can also say, "I can't say yes to that at this time."

Look for the following competencies. If you see these relative emotional highs and lows, ESPECIALLY the underlined competencies, you may have the

CONTROLLER /PUPPET MASTER/PERFECTIONIST PROFILE:

High: <u>reality testing</u>, <u>problem solving</u>, impulse control

Low: <u>flexibility</u>

Take a special look at reality testing, problem solving and flexibility. These are the main indicators of this profile. If you have high impulse control as well, it means that it is highly likely that you have this profile.

Look at self-regard. If self-regard is **low**, you may be a perfectionist who beats yourself up because you don't live up to your own standards. If self-regard is high, you may think that no one else can do it better than you. Either way, people with this profile have a hard time letting go of control and delegating. You may tend to be a workaholic, but are rarely seen as a leader. **This is one of the biggest stumbling blocks to moving past a middle management position.**

Control/Puppet Master/Perfectionist Strengths: Very detail oriented, good at planning and adherence to specifications, high quality work.

How does this Control/Puppet Master/Perfectionist Profile affect the following?:

Time Management: Trouble delegating. You tend to work a lot, but never get everything done. You won't let others do things their way. You won't let them make their mistakes. You are the "go to" problem solver. You stay in the details.

Relationships: You may try to control too many things in relationships, which leads to conflicts. Remember, you can be right or you can be happy.

Team Interaction: You tend to try and control the process and control the direction of the team. Negatively affects collaboration and the team process.

Communication: Preconceptions on how things should be may prevent understanding and connection with others.

Presentation Skills: May be rigid in your approach to presenting. Try being more spontaneous and improvisational. You don't have to have a perfect speech.

Stress Management: Overwhelmed because of lack of delegation. Works too much. Wants to be in on all decisions and know all information and details.

Things to Work On: Flexibility: with yourself, with others, with outcomes. By having a more flexible approach. Delegate more. Ask yourself: Is it wrong, or is it just different? Also, better stress tolerance can be helpful.

Look for the following competencies. If you see these relative emotional highs and lows, ESPECIALLY the underlined competencies, you may have the

ANGER, FRUSTRATION, IMPATIENCE PROFILE:

High: <u>Assertiveness</u>,

Low: <u>Impulse Control</u>, Flexibility

Take a special look at assertiveness and impulse control. These are the main indicators of this profile. If you have low flexibility as well, it means that it is highly likely that you have this profile.

How does this Anger, Frustration, Impatience Profile affect the following?:

Time Management: When experiencing anger, your thinking brain shuts down. This cognitive impairment reduces efficiency.

Relationships: Explosions directed toward others creates negative experiences and diminishes relationships. People won't come to you with anything negative for fear of an explosion.

Team Interaction: Team members may not connect with you. Your explosive nature diminishes interactions.

Communication: Anger, frustration, and impatience limits your communication skills. People will avoid you and not share information because of you over- reactions.

Presentation Skills: May have trouble settling into a calm, easy presentation.

Stress Management: This is a huge factor that adds to stress levels. You are in a low-level fight or flight most of your day, which wears you out. By the end of the day, you are likely exhausted.

Things to Work On: Work on impulse control and empathy. Empathy will decrease assertiveness and impulse control will help with the reactions. Remember, take a deep breath and respond instead of reacting.

If you see the following low scores, you may have the

BURNOUT PROFILE:

Low: self-regard, interpersonal relationships, self-actualization, stress tolerance, optimism, happiness

Five or six out of six = total burnout. Three to four out of six = highly stressed. Two out of six = pay attention. These six competencies contribute to an overall level of happiness and well-being.

Low stress tolerance indicates an inability to handle stressful situations, especially when there are strong emotions involved. You feel overwhelmed and hurried.

NOTE: If you have high stress tolerance, but also are experiencing the physical symptoms of stress (trouble sleeping, headaches or other pain, fatigue, stomach problems, diminished immunity: frequents colds or flu, diminished sex drive, diminished cognitive ability, melancholy or depression) you are racing toward burnout. Just because you have the capacity to cope with stress emotionally doesn't mean it's not taking its toll on your body.

How does this Burnout Profile affect the following?:

Time Management: Don't have the energy to get all of your work done. Overwhelmed, in fight or flight, cognitive processes impaired.

Relationships: Very little time and energy for the relationships in your life and work. May come across as withdrawn and disinterested.

Team Interaction: In survival mode, don't create connections and interactions, also too tired to contribute, you do the minimum.

Communication: Cognitive impairment reduces communication ability. Also, because you are exhausted, you may come across as disinterested.

Presentation Skills: Great presentation is all about energy. When your energy is low, there is no connection with the audience.

Stress Management: Self-explanatory.

Things to Work On: Stress Management is a key here. Build in recovery throughout your day. In addition, if your emotional self-awareness is low, that is the place to begin. You must be able to identify when you are tired, overwhelmed, etc. You must know what is happening in your body. Also, focusing on taking care of yourself, finding purpose and meaning in your life, connecting with others, and cultivating an optimistic outlook will help with this profile.

Look for the following competencies. If you see these relative emotional highs and lows, you may have the

CHAOS, REACTIVE MANAGEMENT PROFILE:

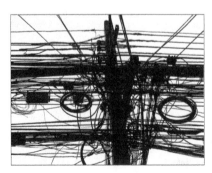

High: Stress Tolerance

Low: Impulse Control

How does this Chaos/Reactive Management Profile affect the following?:

Time Management: You get a lot done, but are just reacting to things. You do not plan proactively. You will usually have low problem-solving skills as well. Work place usually cluttered and cramped.

Relationships: No time for meaningful relationships. Reacts to everything.

Team Interaction: Living in a world of chaos, team interactions are usually frantic and frazzled.

Communication: You don't take the time to cultivate relationships. You may be trying to check emails and work while you are interacting with others.

Presentation Skills: Disorganization contributes to poor presentations.

Stress Management: Always feeling behind, on the treadmill. Feeling stress constantly.

Things to Work On: Increase impulse control while working on managing stress. Remember, respond instead of react.

Look for the following competencies. If you see these relative emotional highs and lows, you may have the

OVERLY OPTIMISTIC PROFILE: Glass half full

High: Optimism Low: Reality Testing

Overly Optimistic strengths: They always think positively about people and situations and sometimes change the outcome.

How does this Overly Optimistic Profile affect the following?:

Time Management: You think you can get more done than you actually can, so you tend to try to schedule too much.

Relationships: People like to be around optimistic, upbeat people. Sometimes over-commitment can lead to misunderstandings and not honoring promises.

Team Interaction: Unrealistic expectations that cannot be met.

Communication: May over-reach with expectations and not communicate clearly with details.

Presentation Skills: Good for presenting. Optimistic, upbeat energy is a magnet.

Stress Management: Mostly good for stress management. Optimistic people tend to cope with stress better, but over-committing and taking on too much may add to stress.

Things to Work On: Would benefit from reality checks with someone you trust. Try to temper your optimism with reality checks and working on your reality testing.

Look for the following competencies. If you see these relative emotional highs and lows, you may have the

PESSIMIST OR REALIST PROFILE: Glass half empty

High: Reality Testing Low: Optimism

Overly Pessimistic Strengths: They bring a reality check to their social and work groups

How does this Pessimist Profile affect the following?:

Time Management: Negative attitude may reduce performance and results. May get mired down in all of the things that are impediments to progress.

Relationships: People shy away from negative people.

Team Interaction: Bring the team down. Be the curmudgeon who always looks at the negative side.

Communication: May take communications down a negative path by focusing on the negative.

Presentation Skills: Audiences may not connect with a negative presentation of a message.

Stress Management: Pessimistic people have higher levels of stress.

Things to Work On: Increase optimism and create more balance. Would benefit from reality checks with someone you trust.

Look for the following competencies. If you see these relative emotional highs and lows, you may have the

TEAM PLAYER PROFILE:

High: Social Responsibility

Low: Independence

Team Player Strengths: Works well in groups or teams.

How does this Team Player profile affect the following?:

Time Management: You may take on too much for the team and not be able to complete your own work.

Relationships: Generally good at relationships, especially in a team setting.

Team Interaction: Excellent with team and collaboration. But may be reluctant to contribute your own ideas.

Communication: Your lower independence may hinder good communication if you hold back saying what is on your mind. But generally, these folks are good communicators.

Presentation Skills: Good presenters. Good connections with audiences.

Stress Management: You may take on too much, which adds to stress levels.

Things to Work On: If there is a large gap between independence and social responsibility (3 points or greater), you may want to work on independence to create some balance. Assertiveness would also be helpful to create the balance.

Look for the following competencies. If you see these relative emotional highs and lows, you may have the

THE LONE WOLF PROFILE:

High: Independence

Low: Social Responsibility

The Lone Wolf Strengths: Can work well alone and be self-motivated.

Lone Wolf Liabilities: Can be held back by lack of motivation to invest in interpersonal potential with others.

How does this Lone Wolf profile affect the following?:

Time Management: Watch isolation that may lead to overwhelm and not relying on others for help.

Relationships: Generally, relationships are not strong.

Team Interaction: Sometimes a good contributor, but usually behind the scenes.

Communication: Without meaningful connections and relationships, sometimes communication is on a superficial level.

Presentation Skills: Generally low energy for presentations and not a great connection with the audience.

Stress Management: Stress levels can be high, especially if you don't ask for help.

Things to Work On: Work on social responsibility and relationships (especially if there is a difference of 3 points or greater on the Ghyst EI Test).

Look for the following competencies. If you see these relative emotional highs and lows, you may have the

CHASES SHINY OBJECTS PROFILE:

High: Flexibility

Low: Impulse Control

Chases Shiny Objects Strengths: Able to embrace something new in a moment's notice.

How does this Chases Shiny Objects profile affect the following?:

Time Management: Generally cluttered workspace. You start more than you finish and go from one thing to the next.

Relationships: You may come across as scattered and unfocused. This may negatively affect relationships.

Team Interaction: Scattered and unfocused, team members may not trust you to complete and contribute.

Communication: Hard to pin down. Unclear communication at times. Unfocused.

Presentation Skills: Presentations seem to be scattered. Goes down rabbit trails and loses the audience.

Stress Management: Stress levels can be high. You rarely slow down and build in recovery.

Things to Work On: Increase impulse control and assertiveness, which will reduce flexibility. Would benefit from learning rhetoric for communication and presentations.

CONTACT INFORMATION

Note: This test and workbook are for individual use only. If you use this for a group or your company, please request permission first.

Test devised by
Dennis Ghyst , Ph.D., Ghyst & Associates
ghystca2@gmail.com
310-221-1334

Contributions on interpretive guidelines by
Brent Darnell/Brent Darnell International
brent@brentdarnell.com
www.brentdarnell.com

System survey contributions
Andrea K Robbins DC ND
docrobbins@naturallybalanced.com

THE FOUR QUADRANTS

The Four Quadrants: Fill in the boxes with words and pictures that represent these areas of your life.

Favorite Piece of Music:

Favorite Quote:

Personal	Work
Family	Personal Future Vision
Perfect Project Outcome	
Personal Challenges	Project Challenges

INSTRUCTIONS:

1. Use flip chart paper (Post it is best) or regular paper for smaller groups. If you have very large groups, you can do this in groups of 4-6. Be sure the groups are totally mixed.

2. Instruct everyone to fill out the four quadrants. They can use pictures or words or whatever they want. This should take around 20 minutes.

3. At the end of the 20 minutes, everyone should present their quadrants one at a time to the group.

4. They can put their flip charts up on the wall and leave them there. Be sure to take photos of each one for future reference. You can go through these several times throughout the project to see what has changed.

5. After each person goes through their information, open it up to the group for any additional questions.

6. Create a project or team playlist from the favorite pieces of music and play this prior to meetings, during lunch, and at team events.

7. This breaks down barriers, creates connections and trust, and a great foundation for collaboration.

BODY BATTERY INVENTORY

 Many stress management seminars talk about reducing the stress in your life. I'm sure there is something to that. But work and life can be very stressful. We take a slightly different approach. Imagine that your body is a battery. There is stress and other things that discharge your body battery and deplete your energy. Those things will always be there. There are also things you can do to recharge your body battery and replenish that energy. So, do your best to decrease the things that are depleting you and increase things that recharge your battery. Try to adjust how you react to stressful situations. If you can build in more ways to recharge your body battery throughout your day, you will have much more energy and be much less stressed at the end of the day.

Fill out the following body battery inventory & plan and see where you are.

Take the tests by placing an "X" on your choice.

Step 1:

Click on the second tab and determine your body battery dischargers.

Step 2:

Click on the third tab to determine your body battery rechargers.

Step 3:

Click on the fourth tab to see your score of the body battery rechargers minus the body battery dischargers.

Step 4:

Still on the fourth tab, fill out your body battery performance plan for daily and occasional stressors and how you will recharge your body battery before, during, or after that stressful event. We include many ways to recharge yourbody battery throughout your day.

	Discharge Body Battery	NONE	SOME	MODERATE	A LOT	INSANE
	Point Value	0	1	2	3	4
1	Work Stress					
2	Personal Stress					
3	Emotional Stress					
4	Travel/Commute Stress					
5	Physical Stress (like training or exercise)					
6	Family Stress					
7	Health Stress (colds, illness, fatigue, etc)					
	Cigarettes per day	0	1-5	6-10	11-15	16+
8	I use nicotine					
	Drinks per week	0	1	2	3	4+
10	I drink alcohol					
	Overweight by lbs	0	5	10	10	16+
12	I am overweight					

Total number of points for dischargers: _____

Physical Symptoms of Stress and Stress Related Illnesses: Put an 'X' next to all that apply to you. These discharge your body battery and deplete your energy.

☐ Headaches: 40 million chronic sufferers

☐ Pain: back, joint, chronic, Fibromyalgia

☐ Fatigue: exhausted at the end of the day, tired when you wake up in the morning, Chronic Fatigue Syndrome

☐ Difficulty sleeping: falling asleep or waking up and can't go back to sleep

☐ Stomach Problems: Acid Stomach, Acid Reflux, Ulcers, Chron's, Irritable Bowel, constipation, diarrhea

☐ Irritability, feeling on the edge, explosive nature, chest pains

☐ Allergies, Asthma, sinus problems

☐ Skin problems (dry skin, eczema, psoriasis, rashes, hives, shingles)

☐ Depression or anxiety: melancholy, no drive, or anxious feelings

☐ Frequent illness, frequent colds or flu, diminished immunity

☐ Cognitive impairment: can't think clearly, memory issues

☐ Diminished sex drive

☐ Diabetes

☐ Arthritis

☐ Cancer

☐ High Blood Pressure

☐ High Cholesterol

☐ Pancreatitis, Lupus, MS, other autoimmune

Multiply the number of physical symptoms/illnesses by 4 _____

Total number of points for stress related symptoms/illnesses: _____

If you have had a major life shift or transition in the past twelve months:

☐ Death of a loved A physical move Graduation

☐ A new job

☐ Being let go from a job Bankruptcy, a failed endeavor Major or life threatening illness Marriage or divorce

☐ A new baby or family member

☐ Any other major life transition or major life stress

Multiply the number of major life shifts by 5 _____

Total number of points for major life shifts: _____

Total number of points: Dischargers, Physical Symptoms of Stress, and Major Life Shifts: This is your Body Battery Discharge Number: _____

Recharge Body Battery	NONE	RARELY	SOMETIMES	MOSTLY	ALL THE TIME
Point Value	**1**	**2**	**3**	**4**	**5**
1 I sleep well and awake refreshed:					
2 I take naps or have complete down time daily:					
3 I have passive recovery times daily [reading (no news or violence), television (no news or violence), movies (no violence or upsetting movies), video games (no violence or upsetting images), music (hopefully soothing and relaxing), radio(no talk radio, news, or violence)]:					
4 I do relaxation exercises for recovery daily (meditation, yoga, breathing, massage):					
5 My diet is filled with nutritious foods and limited simple sugars:					
6 My diet is many small meals spread throughout my day:					
7 I eat only around 1,500 to 2,000 calories per day:					
8 My day has fun in it every day:					
9 I have at least one hour of personal time just for me each day:					
10 I find time for reflection (prayer, meditation, quiet time) each day:					
11 I connect with family, friends, and community daily:					
12 I am grateful and thankful each day:					
13 I take my full two weeks of vacation without checking in at the office:					
14 I have down time every weekend without checking in at the office:					
15 I am positive each day:					
16 I seek rest and recovery every 90 to 120 minutes:					

This is your Body Battery Recharge Number: _____

Body Battery Recharge Number: _____

Body Battery Discharge Number: _____

Body Battery Total Number: _____

If this Body Battery Total Number is positive, keep up the good work. If it is negative or nearly equal, it is recommended that you either find more ways to reduce your body battery discharges or find more ways to recharge your body battery.

See below for your Body Battery Performance Plan. You likely have battery dischargers that deplete your body battery: things such as a daily commute, a daily or weekly meeting, weekly or monthly travel, an annual report, tax time, monthly progress or accounting, bill paying time, stressful family gatherings, encounters with difficult people, etc. These dischargers may be daily or occasional.

Put down the activities that are discharging your body battery and depleting your energy, then fill out what recharging activities you will do before, during, or after to recharge your body battery. The list of 85 battery rechargers are below.

Daily body battery dischargers	Recharging activities

Occasional body battery dischargers	Recharging activities

Sample Body Battery Performance Plan:

Daily body battery dischargers	Recharging activities
commute	music, make weird noises
deadline driven project	positive attitide, take breaks
stressful daily situation	be conciously thankful, smile
meetings, stress at work	deep breathing, turn negative talk into positive
Occasional body battery dischargers	**Recharging activities**
Monthly or Quarterly reports, Meetings	massage, nap, quiet my mind
Paying Bills, April 15th	spend time with my pet, stay hydrated
Holidays	dance, laugh, connect with family
Annual Physical	exercise, drink water, tell jokes

Sample Body Battery Performance Plan:

1. Eat Breakfast and 5 to 6 small meals per day
2. Eat 1,500--2,00 calories per day
3. Have daily connection and support from family, friends and community
4. Be consciously thankful most days
5. Find time to laugh and have fun every day
6. Stay hydrated throughout my day
7. Don't eat many simple, refined sugars
8. Sleep regular hours most nights and get plenty of sleep
9. Take naps when I need to in order to recharge
10. Use caffeine, nicotine and/or alcohol in moderation
11. Exercise regularly (at least 3 times per week)
12. Quiet my mind each day with meditation/prayer/etc
13. Seek rest and recovery every 90 to 120 minutes
14. Take my vacations and enjoy my weekends without checking in at the office or project
15. Maintain a positive attitude even during stressful times.
16. Take five deep breaths.
17. Think of something you are grateful and thankful for.
18. Drink water.

19. Do something silly. Make a face or stick out your tongue.
20. Start a laugh club and laugh daily.
21. Put Scotch tape on your face and distort it.
22. Play hopscotch on the sidewalk.
23. Play a game with kids.
24. Do something extremely physical.
25. Go to an amusement park.
26. Yell at the top of your lungs.
27. Sing or hum a song.
28. Smile. It creates physiological changes.
29. Take a nap.
30. Spend some time with your pet.
31. Go make someone's day with a surprise visit.
32. Change your body.
33. Throw your shoulders back
34. Stretch your arms over your head, then touch your toes
35. Plant your feet firmly on the ground. Feel the heaviness.
36. Feel yourself as you become assertive and powerful.
37. Turn your negative self--talk around.
38. Create a mantra and repeat it.
39. Visualize yourself being relaxed, calm, and full of energy.
40. Dance around the room.
41. Go to a different place physically.
42. Work out with weights or do something that gets your heart rate up.
43. Shake all over like a dog.
44. Get some protein either in shake or bar form.
45. Go for a walk in nature.
46. Call someone who is supportive and talk to them.
47. Look at cool videos or your mind movie.
48. Ask for a hug.
49. Zone out with music.
50. Watch a sitcom or standup comedy show.
51. Take an acting class or a dance class or an aerobics class.
52. Get a massage, acupuncture, reflexology or Reiki.
53. Take an improvisation class.
54. Play nonsense song on the musical instrument of your choice even if you can't play a musical instrument.
55. Tell a joke.

56. Open a window and get some fresh air.
57. Go to some funny websites with jokes or funny videos.
58. Look at a photo of someone you love.
59. Explore your feelings.
60. Doodle, draw a picture.
61. Do the two minute de--stressor: Notice your breath. How are you breathing? Breathe deeply. What are you thinking?
62. Are there thoughts that cause this stress? Think of things you are grateful and thankful for. Tap the tip of your tongue on the gums just above the top front teeth.
63. Look in Stress Tolerance section of the Total Leadership Program Resource book.
64. Read a kid's book.
65. Look at fish in an aquarium.
66. Look at birds, squirrels and other animals near your house.
67. Look under a rock and observe what is there.
68. Go to a museum or aquarium.
69. Help someone in need.
70. Visit an assisted living place and sing a song for the residents.
71. Have lunch at Chucky Cheese or other kid's restaurant.
72. Have a mindful meal that lasts at least one hour.
73. Make faces in the mirror.
74. Give yourself a massage on your shoulders and face.
75. Take a Jacuzzi.
76. Run as fast as you can.
77. Try to not think about zebras.
78. Put on some disco and do the robot.
79. Pretend to be someone else.
80. Make weird noises.
81. Do a puzzle.
82. Make a prank phone call to a friend.
83. Eat an ice cream cone or frozen yogurt.
84. Get a mani pedi (that's manicure and pedicure).
85. Gargle sing a song or burp the alphabet.
86. Strike a Power Pose (hands on hips, hands up in the air, spread yourself out and take up a lot of space) for 2 minutes. This will increase your testosterone by 20% and decrease your cortisol (the stress hormone) by 15% from the baseline. For more information, Google Amy Cuddy Ted Power Pose.

OUTCOME COACHING

Ask these questions of the other person whether this is an inner conflict or conflict with another person or persons. If this is an inner conflict, skip the highlighted questions. After each question, explore more possibilities by saying, "Tell me more about that." or "Let's explore that in a little more detail.".

Current Reality:
1. What is the issue?
2. What have you done about it to date? Was there a response from the other person or persons?
3. What do you want?
4. What do they want?
5. What are the stumbling blocks? For you? For them?

Future Vision:
1. What is the perfect, desired outcome?
2. Put yourself in the other person's shoes. How do they see it? What do they want?
3. Helicopter view: Fly above this situation as an observer. Does this perspective change your viewpoint?
4. May I ask some questions/give you some advice (keep in mind it's just my opinion)?
5. Are any of these ideas sounding good to you? Enough to take action on?

Step-by-step:
1. What would be the first step to move this forward to a conclusion?
2. What is the next step after that? After that?
3. What are the obstacles for you? For them?
4. How can you overcome these obstacles? How do you think they can overcome these obstacles?

Follow up and changing future behaviors:
1. How will you know when this issue is resolved?
2. What did you learn from this process?
3. What will you do differently going forward/next time?

PRIMAL SAFETY TOOLBOX SAFETY TOPICS

The toolbox safety meetings should be fun and informative. You should not only discuss best safety practices, rules, and regulations, but address the emotional side of safety as well. We recommend walking safety meetings and mini-safety meetings. Walk around in large or small groups and point out safety issues like housekeeping, working from heights, scaffold and ladder safety, barriers and handrails, personal protective equipment, and any other safety topics that you find to be relevant. Ask them for their input. Ask them what they see. Ask them to point out what is wrong.

1. Stretch every morning. Have some theme from Rocky or James Brown I Feel Good playing.

2. Pair up. Have everyone introduce themselves and tell about their family (whatever that definition is for them).

3. Pair up. Get back to back. Remove a piece of safety equipment. Face each other and see if you can guess what is missing.

4. Get in small groups and discuss the potential dangers for the day and how to overcome them.

5. Walk around in small groups and have everyone point out potentially unsafe areas and situations.

6. Celebrate everyone's birthday for each month and give each person a small gift. At lunch, have a big sheet cake for everyone.

7. Pair up. Tell each other why it's important that you go home safely that day.

8. Tell a story about a near miss or a save and what it meant to that person.

9. Hand out Primal Safety Coloring books and crayons. Have their kids color the pages, laminate the pages and put them up around the project.

10. Discuss the importance of glucose in your brain and decision making.

11. Tell everyone to take five deep breaths and relax. A non-stressed brain makes better decisions.

12. Pair up. Tell each other a lifelong dream that you have.

13. Pair up. Tell each other a family story.

14. Pair up. Ask each other, "Why is it important that you work safely?"

15. Pair up. Tell each other what would happen if they went to work today without any personal protective equipment on.

16. Discuss how stress shuts down your thinking brain and keeps you from making good decisions.

17. Hand out some healthy snacks for the day like some nuts or healthy protein bars.

18. Show the group an unsafe situation or scenario and see if they can come up with an intervention and solution. Make it a contest.

19. Actually show how a harness can protect against a fall.

20. Tell everyone how dehydration affects them: Increased thirst, dry mouth, swollen tongue, weakness, dizziness, palpitations, confusion, sluggishness, fainting, no sweat, decreased urine.

21. Celebrate a safety milestone with a short party with food.

22. Read an obituary from someone who died on a construction project and what family was left behind.

23. Have everyone take the Ghyst EI Test and discuss how their profile can affect safety.

24. Tell them that if they are working unsafely, you will send them home and they can't return until they have a note from their spouse or family member.

25. Discuss how their judgment can be impaired from lack of sleep.

26. Discuss how their judgment can be impaired from drugs (OTC, prescription, recreational).

27. Discuss how good nutrition will not only positively affect performance, but they will also live a longer, healthier life.

28. Discuss why they are so tired at the end of the day: poor nutrition, poor sleep, not enough breaks, dehydration, holding muscles in tension, distracted thoughts, energy vampires (people who suck the life out of you). Also discuss how you can reduce these.

29. Discuss safety and alpha males and how this hypermasculine environment is not good for safety. A caring environment yields much better safety and productivity numbers.

30. Have everyone tell how they celebrate Holidays.

31. Have everyone tell how they celebrate birthdays.

32. Have everyone tell how they celebrate becoming an adult.

33. Tap into a larger purpose for your project and create a family work environment where everyone values and cares for each other.

34. Have everyone tell about how their kids reacted to The Primal Safety Coloring Book.

35. Have everyone tell each other that they want them to go home safely today.

36. Pair off. Tell each other how you overcame a struggle during childhood.

37. Have everyone jump up and down 10 times. Get the energy up for a safe day.

38. Have everyone discuss how their mental state (stressed, angry, etc.) affects safety.

39. Have everyone discuss the importance of taking breaks.

40. Have everyone discuss the importance of not working while tired or hungry.

41. Discuss how mobile phones can be distracting and unsafe while working.

42. Use mobile phones during the meeting to call or text a loved one and let them know that you will work safely that day.

43. Discuss how safety can increase productivity.

44. Discuss how organization and cleanup can affect attitudes and safety.

45. Have everyone get into small groups and tell a joke or good story.

46. Show what multi-tasking is a myth. It's really multi-switching and it is not good for high levels of safety. Tell them to count to 24 by 2s. Then spell multitasking. Time each one. Then tell them to alternate them: 2, m, 4, u, 6, l, etc. Time that. It usually takes two to three times longer.

47. Have everyone shut their eyes and do a visualization of a safe day and what it looks like.

48. Pair off. Have everyone tell a story about the kids in their life.

49. Pair off. Have everyone tell a story about how they met their spouse or partner. If they don't have a partner, tell them to tell a story about how they met their best friend.

50. Have a discussion on what family means and what it means to look out for each other.

51. Pair off. Have everyone discuss how they would teach their kids about how to use their personal protective equipment.

52. Have a discussion about the future, such as their life five years from now or when they retire and what they hope to accomplish.

CPSIA information can be obtained
at www.ICGtesting.com
Printed in the USA
BVHW091438070121
596914BV00001B/1